HEALING DEATH

HEALING DEATH

Finding the healing to live well into our dying

By
CHRISTOPHER LEVAN

CASCADE *Books* • Eugene, Oregon

HEALING DEATH
Finding the healing to live well into our dying

Copyright © 2020 Christopher Levan. All rights reserved. Except for brief quotations in critical publications or reviews, no part of this book may be reproduced in any manner without prior written permission from the publisher. Write: Permissions, Wipf and Stock Publishers, 199 W. 8th Ave., Suite 3, Eugene, OR 97401.

Cascade Books
An Imprint of Wipf and Stock Publishers
199 W. 8th Ave., Suite 3
Eugene, OR 97401

www.wipfandstock.com

PAPERBACK ISBN: 978-1-5326-9525-4
HARDCOVER ISBN: 978-1-5326-9526-1
EBOOK ISBN: 978-1-5326-9527-8

Cataloguing-in-Publication data:

Names: Levan, Christopher.
Title: Healing death : finding the healing to live well into our dying / Christopher Levan.
Description: Eugene, OR: Cascade Books, 2020 | Includes bibliographical references.
Identifiers: ISBN 978-1-5326-9525-4 (paperback) | ISBN 978-1-5326-9526-1 (hardcover) | ISBN 978-1-5326-9527-8 (ebook)
Subjects: LCSH: Right to die | Ethics, medical | Euthanasia | Euthanasia—religious aspects.
Classification: R726 .L374 2020 (print) | R726 (ebook)

Manufactured in the U.S.A.   SEPTEMBER 10, 2020

Dedicated to Tia Levan, a daughter-in-law, who holds and changes our hearts and minds

Those who claim they can always alleviate the suffering of the dying have either not had enough exposure to the problem or are lacking in a simple quality: compassion.

—Dr. Christiaan Barnard
Good Life, Good Death: A Doctor's Case for Euthanasia

I choose medical assistance in death because I love and cherish life. For me life is to be lived as Thoreau described: "deliberately.... I did not wish to live what was not life, living is so dear.... I wanted to live deep and suck out all the marrow of life."

—Martine Partridge
in a letter to her family and friends, explaining her decision to seek medical assistance to end her life. *Calgary Sun*, June 16, 2017

CONTENTS

Acknowledgments | ix

Introduction: Death Is Not the Enemy | 1

Chapter 1
Five Facts About Medical Assistance in Dying | 16

Chapter 2
Our Spiritual Heritage | 31

Chapter 3
Advancing Our Living or Prolonging Our Dying | 48

Chapter 4
Curing the Disease vs. Healing the Illness | 59

Chapter 5
Healing Death | 72

Chapter 6
Cautions: The Defense of the Vulnerable | 77

Chapter 7
Recommendations: A Funeral Rehearsal | 83

Appendix 1: Definition of ALS | 89
Appendix 2: Bill C-14 | 94

Bibliography | 111

ACKNOWLEDGMENTS

I began this research with the click of a mouse. It was early spring 2016, and the high holidays were approaching. Passion week for Christians is the season when the cross looms large. The predictable Good Friday sermon was inviting me into the valley of the shadow again. And I thought the Internet might have some light to shed on the debate around medical assistance in dying, which was prominently featured in the news of that year. The deadline for federal legislation responding to the Supreme Court decision on the Carter case[1] was closing in on the Canadian Parliament. In that decision, the country's highest court upheld the right for some individuals under certain circumstances to have medical assistance in dying.

At the time, I thought I knew what I believed: contrary to the federal court's opinions, I saw this step as a thoughtless and potentially dangerous capitulation to liberal individualism. Life is a gift not a possession. We are stewards of our living, not owners, and to usurp the role of Creator and fashion our own ending is the height of hubris. How can we take what is essentially a gift and turn it into personal property to be discarded at will? To think we have a right to control everything was absurd. God holds out some

---

1. The "Carter" case refers to the constitutional challenge put forward by the family of Lee Carter et al., of British Columbia, which resulted in the Supreme Court decision that mandated a change to the Criminal Code, essentially decriminalizing medical assistance in dying.

ACKNOWLEDGMENTS

surprises in life, and those unknowns are often the source of great miracles. Theologically, I was opposed.

Ethically, I was worried for our common life. Our society changes when we gift the power over life onto individual hands. We are a new people when something that had been forbidden suddenly becomes a "right." At first glance, medical assistance in dying offers a compassionate, dignified end to insufferable pain. However, it also removes the absoluteness of living, no matter the circumstance. So, what presents itself as benevolence for the intolerably sick also places many other people at risk, for there is no longer an *a priori* justification for life. It's now a matter of choice. And the more vulnerable of our society—the elderly, the differently abled—will now have to argue for the merits of their continued existence.

That was my thinking . . . at the time.

To prepare for my sermon, I was driving down the electronic highway looking for websites and ideas to support my opinions. (Isn't that what we all do? The World Wide Web is a mirror. We surf the net to find ourselves?) And while there was no lack of sites trumpeting my cause—home pages with helpful biblical passages attached, all condemning the preemptive ending of human life—the more I searched, the more I was drawn deeper and deeper into the reality of human pain. And that changed everything.

Of course, there are whole libraries on death. Likewise, there is a mushrooming stack of published articles on dying with dignity—especially since Bill C-14, the Canadian federal legislation of dying with medical assistance, was enacted. Keeping track of the increasing number of online podcasts and blogs, which explore personal experiences at the hospital bedside, could be a full-time job.

It was one, pre-Bill C-14 article on an older woman's painstaking journey to end her life, not involving her partner who might otherwise be charged with a criminal act, that was so poignant, so heart-wrenching, that I felt drawn to work harder at my own position. It was a story told from a time before the current legislation was even considered. In this woman's context, there was considerable risk to those who might consider helping anyone end their life. Several well-meaning individuals had previously found themselves charged with accessory to murder under the criminal code. I read how, even while terribly crippled, this individual was obliged to drag a mattress by herself down to her "sacred place," the one that afforded her a view in front of her country home. She arranged her method of ending her life on her own, not involving a soul, so no one could be accused of colluding to take her life. Her ending was a solitary act, painful, and, in many ways, nobly tragic! The family watched helplessly as she struggled to do everything on her own. That story struck me deeply, and I felt, surely we can do better than this. Quite separate from my church's position or my personal opinions, this kind of anguish was unconscionable. If our end is close and nothing remains but crippling suffering, must we force people into such devious and grievous manipulations in order to accomplish what seems to make so much sense?

From that single story has grown a year's worth of reading. I began asking how death could be a healing process, and it was through this study that I began to understand why our current vocabulary about and models for celebrating the end of life are inadequate.

During this research, I have heard many similar stories of great courage and compassion. So let me begin by acknowledging how honored and grateful I am to those who have been so open in sharing their stories of great emotion, distress, and physical pain. I am humbled by their spiritual strength. In all the cases I encountered, medical assistance in dying was not used as an easy escape, not a cheap evasion of human responsibility to live fully with the gift God has given. On the contrary, those who came to the place of using medical assistance in dying were doing so as the faithful way to complete their life. In equal measure, those who opposed medical assistance in dying were highly compassionate, aware of the pain that many suffer at the end. They were deeply moved by the need to offer care and compassion at the end, while refusing to hasten that end in any way. The debate proved to be as complex and as lively as any I could imagine, and this book will hopefully reflect that complexity, avoiding simplistic responses while offering some pathways forward.

I recall, distinctly, the debate I had with my daughter-in-law, Tia. She was clear, coming from her hard-nosed common sense. She asked me if I was in favor of "making people suffer? Surely not! If you could heal them of that anguish, wouldn't you?" It was Tia who helped me to realign my thinking, seeing medical assistance in dying as compassionate "healing" rather than as orchestrated "suicide."

In addition to the many individuals who contributed to this project, I would like to thank Robert Oliphant, the co-chair of the parliamentary committee that studied this issue and presented their report, which was used in the establishing of the legislation, Bill C-14. Rob's intellectual leadership, his theological and ethical insights, have been invaluable. I am especially grateful for his work with groups of religious leaders . . . both in listening to their alternate points of view and in presenting his own.

It was through the Louisville Institute of Louisville, Kentucky, that this research received its primary support. Their sympathy to a uniquely Canadian reality and their very professional and sympathetic response to my ideas have been invaluable. Through their financial generosity and moral support, I was given the time and resources to research and write. I am so thankful.

When I explained my work to a colleague in Cuba, his response was to comment on how giving my local congregation had been. "They let you do all this study?" he asked. "They are certainly generous!" And so they are!—grace-filled and encouraging. I owe a great deal to College Street United Church in Toronto for their healing and forgiveness . . . both of which have brought me home to my primary vocation, which is to write.

I am writing this section of the book at the country inn of my closest friends, Ann Vickers and Ray Drennan. If I turn to the left, I can look out to the bay at Bouchtouche, New Brunswick. For the peace of their home and their constant encouragement . . . not to mention the whiskey . . . I am always so thankful. Likewise, I

ACKNOWLEDGMENTS

owe an eternal debt of gratitude to Bronwyn Best who edits and improves my words and thoughts.

Finally, to my wife, Ellen. Thank you so much. I am so grateful to you, because you taught me to laugh at myself and yet to take every minute of living with a deep seriousness. In our short time together, we've walked down some pretty crazy and beautiful pathways. There is no other life we are given, and when we come to our last day, surely it should have as much meaning as those days which preceded it. Sometimes, we think safety is found in guarding ourselves and our hearts, but Ellen has taught me the joyous, wild truth of the aria she sings from Carmen: "Si je t'aime, prends garde à toi."

Bouchtouche, May 2017

Introduction

DEATH IS NOT THE ENEMY

Most of our simple wisdom can be found on a T-shirt, if we look hard enough. Last week, as I was preparing to write the first pages of this book, on a clearance rack in the local general store, I found this: "Death: The #1 Killer in the World." Perhaps that slogan captures the basic premise of my research: everyone dies.

When I taught undergraduates, I would begin a series of lectures on religious and philosophical attitudes to death and dying with two simple affirmations: "First, there is one thing every human being will accomplish. We will all manage to die. We can take great comfort in the fact that even if we are lazy, inept, devious or delusional, every one of us will complete the dying task perfectly. It's a sure bet. Second, dying is the only thing you can count on doing on your own. No one joins you on this journey. People may stand by your side, even hold your hand, but unlike any other human act, including birth, you will walk through that door, naked, vulnerable and absolutely alone."[1]

---

1. We are alone, in one sense. There is no other human being that walks with us through death. However, I am convinced by the United Church New Creed, which affirms that we are never alone: "In life, in death, in life beyond death, God is with us. We are not alone."

HEALING DEATH

Perhaps death is the single fact which unites us as a species. Forget love or faith, family ties or collective memory. Our chief, unifying characteristic is our dying. Among the creatures on earth, we are perhaps one of the few species that knows we will end. Am I presuming too much? Who knows what a dog might think, for instance?² But there is no doubt that as living beings we are shaped by our dying, and our high level of consciousness as creatures is a result of our keen awareness of our undeniable ending. From a very young age, we are led into that dark reality by fairy tales and the stories told in our sacred books. A quick read of such divergent stories as Hansel and Gretel and John's gospel shows just how central are the themes of death and dying—our anxiety over the darkness and our search for freedom from the abyss. As we move from childhood into adolescence, we continue to test the edges of our fear about dying, through graphic novels and horror flicks—even experimenting with real life, role-play video games and battles. And all the Disney movies notwithstanding, at an early age, we realize that life does not continue "happily ever after." It just ends. At some point in my life, my friends and I will journey out into the cemetery, and they will leave me there alone and go back to what is left of their lives. I will simply not be!

The T-shirt is right—death is the #1 killer in the world. It will catch us all, from presidents to paupers. No one will avoid it. And that finality causes unending anxiety and conflict. Who wants to think of their end, of not being? When we are young, we imagine we are immortal, but as we walk through year after year, we come to a rising awareness that the grim reaper waits for no one. And as the quantity of days diminishes, the quality of each passing moment rises—making our ending all the more poignant.

The vast fear and trembling we experience as beings fuels a whole industry of youth-crazed, anti-aging products and activities.³ Everything from skin cream to skydiving is sold to us as a

---

2. One of the most moving commentaries on dying is a fictional letter written by a dog to his master and mistress produced by the American playwright Eugene O'Neill, *Last Will and Testament*. A great bedtime story.

3. See Kierkegaard, *Fear and Trembling*, in which he explains the process of

cure for death. How strange, to expend such tremendous amounts of energy avoiding what we all know is inevitable! Much of our despair as teenagers or our depression as elders can be traced back to this great limit to human life. It was existential philosophy that reminded us how we are finite creatures. We either despair that we are never going to find meaning within the circumscribed time we have been given—which is perhaps the chief anxiety of the postmodern age—or we sense, as many millennials do, that this life is not worth the energy, given the finality of death that hangs over us.

And if we dissect our fear more carefully, we realize that it is not the actual event of dying that haunts us—though that can be disconcerting. The black hole of nonbeing waiting on the other side of death is a mystery that nags at us. Yes. However, most humans are more disturbed by the process of dying. As Woody Allen puts it, "I am not afraid of death; I just don't want to be there when it happens."[4] It's the way we must enter our dying that can cause nightmares. Will it be gentle and calm or pain wracked and unrelenting? Can I remain me, preserve some dignity at the end, or will I be stripped of my humanity, left helpless and groveling?[5] As a pastor, I have seen far too many folk drool away their final days, sucking on an oxygen tube, wetting the bed and totally lost to themselves and others. How do I protect my heart and soul against such an ending? As my mind and body deteriorate, my chief concern is my dignity. And my dignity is knotted up with my personal agency and emotional integrity. Why can't I just order up a midsleep, subdural aneurism?[6] That way, I go to sleep whole and hardy

---

coming to faith as the total relinquishment of self and self-will.

4. See: https://www.goodreads.com/quotes/2989-i-m-not-afraid-of-death-i-just-don-t-want-to.

5. One of the most haunting ballads about war is entitled "Green Fields of France," written by Eric Bogle. We hear the haunting fear of how we die in the first verse, which is an introduction to a random soldier, Willie McBride, who died in Flanders. That verse reads: "Well I hope you died quick and I hope you died clean, or Willie McBride was it slow and obscene?"

6. Apparently, only about five percent of us will be granted the death during sleep scenario. The rest of us will face the grim reaper with eyes wide open.

and simply never awaken. The uncertainty of how we will die is the source of our anxiety.

And that is the dominant motivator for so many I have interviewed with respect to medical assistance in dying. We have watched our parents pass. Weeks, even years, of visits to the nursing home haunt us with images of lost souls who quite literally waste away their final months, sitting alone in a windowless hallway, mouths gapping, eyes vacant. "Not me," we say firmly. How often in the past year of research has someone told me that they don't want to be a forgotten vegetable in a lonely room? "Stand on the air tube" will be written above my bed.

We could describe this aspect of our fear as the decline of control. And while death is the ultimate act of relinquishing our personal agency, our dying is also intertwined with our human dignity and the loss of identity. No one wants to be reduced to a disease: to be nothing more than a cancer-ridden body. And we all fear being robbed of the most essential part of living: our sense of self; our ability to love and be loved. Alzheimer's is the ultimate insult, because it robs us of who we are and yet does not kill us quickly. "I" am forced to continue living, even while the "I" is gone.

Then there is pain—perhaps the most important factor in the current debate. We all fear the end, because of the agony it might entail. No one should have to suffer unduly, and public sympathy is clearly opposed to prolonging a person's anguish. How often have we told ourselves that our society condones putting dogs, cats, horses, our loved animals, to sleep rather than have them suffer? Our compassion says it's "the right thing to do." Indeed, it was because of the unrelenting suffering of several people, notably Sue Rodriguez and Lee Carter, that we have the legislation on medical assistance in dying. It was their pain that propelled their cases all the way to the Supreme Court of Canada.

While many people approach their end with relatively little discomfort, those who suffer will tell you of how it distorts everything. This we fear more than anything else: the lingering torture of a vicious cancer, as it eases its way through vital organs, the bone-on-bone grinding of degenerative arthritis, the mental anguish of seeing your body become more and more immobilized, while your mind is still vital and awake, the desperate grasping for every breath as one slowly suffocates, the loss of bodily functions. Everyone can imagine the horrors of a painful ending. And we fear it.

It is to alleviate this pain that we now have medical assistance in dying. And while some palliative care pain clinics offer solace and the promise of relief,[7] many Canadians outside major urban centers have no access to such services. And those who suffer unrelenting pain will tell you that it is life-altering. It racks the body, but takes over the mind and soul as well. It clouds everything. As Betty told me, "Pain can cloud your mind so much that it fills your mind with a 'pain fog.'"[8]

And aside from our fear of nonbeing and the pain associated with dying, there is yet another aspect of death that keeps us awake at night: the solitary nature of dying. It is as disturbing as the pain we might suffer. There is no way around it. I must enter into my end on my own. No matter how much I am loved, and how many companions I have made along this pilgrimage, death is a one-person show. And the singularity of dying haunts me. If my chief anxiety during life is the desire to be part of a community, to be accepted and included, then to be totally alone is a very frightening prospect. And this fact about dying retrojects back into our living a serious doubt over our ultimate meaning and purpose. What if I don't really matter? If there is no grand finale to my life,[9] is it possible I am nothing more than a haphazard, a basically pointless being? What if there is no heaven-sent plan, no providential plot giving shape and purpose to my life? Could I be meaningless? Is it possible that, in the end, I am not important at all, not part of anything majestic or grand, but just a singular, randomly contingent animal? The prospect of dying raises these troubling questions.

---

7. See the groundbreaking work of a United Church member and doctor, Balfour Mount, in Montreal at https://en.wikipedia.org/wiki/Balfour_Mount.

8. Quote from an interview with Betty Mittler, June 2017, 10:20 a.m.

9. This is the haunting message of an old, classic music movie, *All That Jazz*.

Dying, while it often follows a predictable pattern, is, nonetheless, a complex event, as our biological self interacts with our spiritual and emotional desires.[10] Yet it comes to all, despite our will or ability as a species. It's built right into the cycle of creation. The day we are born, we start the march toward our grave. And while advances in medical science and technological prowess have meant that human beings can manipulate greater and greater aspects of their living, there is no antidote to dying, no elixir of eternal life. As the song lyric puts it: "If ever I leave this world alive."[11] There's no way out of this finite world except through death.

And it is, therefore, surprising that we have a reticence to talk about death openly. It's the monster in the closet, the boogeyman under the bed. We don't spend much time preparing for or thinking about it until it's often too late. As the dark secret we all keep, it also holds a fascination for the modern mind as entertainment. So, even though death holds our imaginations, it does not invite casual conversation or reveal itself easily. So, we have to organize special gatherings and coffee encounters.[12] Radio programmes invite listeners to tell their stories of grief.[13] All this work to unmask the devil we call death.

Death Is Not the Enemy

From the beginning of my conversations with those who have worked through the process of medical assistance in dying, I was told a simple fact: death is not the enemy we imagine. During a conversation with Ethel Campbell, I heard how her daughter, Julia,

---

10. One of the best explorations of the process of dying is found in *Good Life, Good Death*, by Christiaan Barnard.

11. The tune is sung by Flogging Molly.

12. Look up http://deathcafe.com/. There is a growing movement called "Death Café," whose stated objective is to talk about death. "At a Death Cafe people, often strangers, gather to eat cake, drink tea and discuss death. Our objective is 'to increase awareness of death with a view to helping people make the most of their (finite) lives.'" See more at: http://deathcafe.com/what/#sthash.FofSqmoY.dpuf.

13. Maritime noon program CBC, May 18, 2017, 12–1 PM.

who was assisted in her death on July 20, 2016, greeted death as a friend. Julia was living with ALS and had suffered much. The family was on a 24/7 watch. Julia went through the incredible pain of a disintegrated shoulder and other physical agony because of her disease. In the end, she could only communicate by blinking her eyes. However, with conviction, she telegraphed her desires, and through the dedication of her family, she was able to end her life with dignity. She dictated a letter to her sister, who read it on the day of her dying . . . family and friends gathered on the back deck and people could say good-bye and offer gratitude for Julia's life while she was still able to hear them. Ethel told me that Julia's death was a healing moment. Though painful and heart-wrenching, it was also a "gift of life back to us," for it freed the family from the constant vigilance and care and sense of helplessness, as they watched their loved one decline.[14] For Julia and her family, death was not the enemy but a welcome step on the journey of living.

It was from Ethel and many others that I began to understand that dying, an essential part of living, might also be a healing moment. And that fact raised many pastoral questions that became the guiding ideas of my research and writing. They are: If dying is neither an exceptional event nor the enemy of living but a part of life, how can we shape our encounter with death so that it becomes a welcome, meaningful end? Since death is clearly part of what it means to be human, shall we not apply as much calm intentionality to dying as we do to living? Is it not possible to walk through our dying in such a way that we have been healed?

In the end, the guiding thesis of this text became a simple affirmation. We can place the words "healing" and "death" together in the same sentence, for it is possible that, in our ending, we can experience a wholeness and completion which is quite restorative.

It may seem like a contradiction to talk of dying as a healing process. On the surface, they seem to be opposites. Isn't death a defeat? It is the triumph of the shadows that threaten us: the victory

---

14. Taken from an interview held with Ethel Campbell on April 10, 2017, 12 PM.

of "that good night."[15] The light is snuffed out by the grave and the downfall of all efforts for curing the diseases that take away our life. How can there be healing in death? This book will explore the many ways in which our manner of dying can be a road to healing.

A simple example at this point will suffice to illustrate how we will explore death as a form of healing. How often have I stood at the graveside, saying good-bye to a beloved father or mother, and there in the circle of mourners is a space where the youngest son or the oldest daughter should be standing. They weren't welcome. No one wants to talk about it, for fear of "upsetting" the ceremony, but there's an open wound that needs addressing. And while it is not within my ability to heal it during the funeral itself, it is a pity that, in the time leading up to a parent's death, we lacked the rituals or traditions which might have allowed for the reconciliation of this broken relationship. We don't have the tradition or the means of acknowledging and forgiving our missteps and mistakes! Surely, at our end, this is one of our chief desires and tasks. Death wins, when we allow it to rob us of the chance to be reunited with the very precious, but broken, bits and pieces of our life.

In the past, the possibility of finding healing in our dying was confounded by the uncertainty surrounding the event. No one knows when it will happen, at least not with anything like precision. So, we let it slide. The young son will come home eventually. No need to push it or presume. That older daughter will come when "it's time." And planning a healthy, wholesome ending to our life feels either like capitulation to fatalism or a macabre self-absorption. Those who are dying don't want to call attention to themselves, and those who are in the dying person's circle don't want to plan anything, lest they look like they are prematurely pushing the dying person into their grave.

Besides, dying is, by its nature, a confusing and conflicting time. Any bent or broken emotions we have carried during our life get crazier as we close in on the end. There are only a few noble examples of clarity in our dying: Socrates drinking hemlock with his

---

15. Taken from Dylan Thomas' poem: "Do Not Go Gentle Into That Good Night," first published in the journal *Botteghe Oscure* in 1951.

friends around about his bed or Jesus speaking with his disciples in the upper room.[16] But such examples appear to be exceptions—quite exotic and seemingly impossible to emulate. It's easier to let things ride. Only a very few courageous ones can plan their ending with healing in mind.[17]

The new legal situation in Canada in which certain individuals can avail themselves of medical assistance in dying changes everything. It is now possible that some individuals could plan and prepare for their end with every expectation that it would happen within their control, that it would bring healing and offer greater hope and peace to those who are left behind. And while medical assistance in dying raises many complex ethical and spiritual dilemmas, it also offers the possibility to implement rituals and traditions that will bring healing to death. The latter portion of this text will examine what these rituals might be and how healing might take place.

A Good Death and a Bad Death

When asked, most religious leaders will confess that their best pastoral moments come during funerals. Most of us would much rather lead people through the valley of the shadow than down the aisle to a wedding.
At the graveside, we sense that matters are more real and human, since there tends to be less pretending when death is a visitor in the room. And we have been witness to both good and bad death.

During this research, I have been honored to hear the stories of the dying and have been given permission to make some of these tales public. Here's a marvelous story of the good death.

---

16. There is nothing to equal the words of Jesus expressed in the gospel of John 14:1. It is on Maundy Thursday, and he spends his final hours before his crucifixion with his disciples: "Let not your hearts be troubled, believe in God, believe also in me."

17. An excellent, modern version of the planned, noble death was written by Kelly, *Chasing Daylight*.

Kathryn told me of Sandy, her sister's sister-in-law, who was living with ALS and was unable to continue.

Sandy decided to ask for medical assistance in dying. Having been given a permission and date, not only was she able to meet with friends and share some final words, she was able to invite her grandchildren to join her for one last shopping trip. Sandy loved to window shop, and so they all went to the mall, relived memories of past trips, and did some serious people watching while reveling in the life that was so evident in passersby. These grandchildren told their grandmother how important she was, how much of a difference she had made in their young lives. Finally, Sandy's husband joined them for lunch, and then Sandy went home to die, content she had closed the circle and left her offspring with one final memory.[18]

Can you picture this scene? It seems so simple and unremarkable, but alas, it doesn't happen often. Perhaps we should take a pause here. Take a deep breath and ponder how unique and yet how important it is to praise an elder for their love. And more, to know that they have heard us. Imagine this! In Sandy's case, this leave-taking was a lively dialogue rather than the less satisfying monologue that characterizes most funerals. A granddaughter sat beside her and spoke of her love. Of course, Sandy knew she was loved, but now her granddaughter knew that Sandy had heard clearly how important that was. Is there any better way to complete the circle of compassion?

A good death!

After Kathryn finished telling the story, I was blessed with a vision . . . this is how dying can be a healing moment. ALS finally killed Sandy, but she died a healed woman, leaving behind children and grandchildren, who did not deny death or pretend it away but who incorporated it into their living. The model of this good death gave me a vision of how we might establish a better ritual practice around our dying.

---

18. Comments recorded from a phone interview with Kathryn, May 10, 2017, at 9 PM.

In tragic contrast, I officiated at a funeral many years ago, where everyone was speechless. The actual ceremony was not exceptional—a polished casket, a large crowd, many words of gratitude and a good measure of grief. It was the potluck after the internment that was unsettling. This woman had died as she lived, denying most facts and manipulating those around her to do the same. There had been no succession planning, no final reckoning, no farewells or forgiveness. Many of the damaging dynamics of the family had been perpetuated. I could taste the animosity sparking from one side of the table to the other. It was only after that I realized the seating had not been random—the family had quite literally lined up against each other—one side of the table refusing to co-operate with the other. There was a daughter-in-law who refused to take part in anything, an ex-partner of one of the children who had co-opted the role of host and made sure to stir the pot with old memories. No one could venture a reconciling gesture, and everyone spoke of the deceased in completely one-dimensional ways for fear of causing an argument. Rather than closing the circle and bringing resolution, the funeral was like the starter's pistol shot announcing a new race of recrimination.

As I sat eating my scraps of ham, I thanked my lucky stars that I had only to offer a prayer at their dinner and did not have to stick around for the reading of the will, which one of the siblings had produced with great flair. Let the battle begin . . . again!

This was a bad death. There was no healing in this person's dying, but just a perpetuation of the discomfort and hard feelings that had characterized her living.

Finding a Path to Healing

It is to offer alternatives to such a "bad death" that I present this text. Of course, human beings are not programmable. We cannot always avoid the contradictions and contingencies that cause us anguish and pain. Blind self-absorption and power-hungry enmity cannot be cured by a few words, no matter how well chosen. Likewise, the bent dynamics of a family will not be healed by medical assistance in dying. After all, people spend a whole lifetime creating their own unique problems. The few brief days preparing for death will not alter those troubles very much. But, perhaps some broken relationships can be restored with adequate planning and reflection.

This text is offered as a guide to the current new situation. As mentioned above, it posits the possibility that death can be a healing moment. To explain this proposition, the first chapter will lay the groundwork for the current legislative and pastoral situation. There are essentially five sets of facts to consider as a background to the thesis that dying is a healing moment in human living. First, we must take into account the historical background to the new legislation, Bill C-14. To do this, we'll explore a brief history of the two legal challenges which resulted in a change in the Criminal Code. In the second place, it is essential that we familiarize ourselves with the actual regulations that govern medical assistance in dying. It may come as an unsettling surprise what is and what is not actually covered by this legislation. A third "fact," is the role health care professionals play in implementing medical assistance in dying. The legislation has been written to place a great deal of discretion and responsibility on their shoulders. And, currently, the response from medical professionals has been inconsistent across the country. A fourth factor raised by some people I have interviewed is the structural discrepancies and inadequacies faced by those who seek medical assistance in dying. This is such a new "procedure" or "service" that we do not have a consistent way of implementing and supporting it. Our health system has been oriented in the opposite direction: the preservation of life. To contemplate and plan for death runs against the grain of much health care training, and consequently, it appears initially more like a defeat than a solution. Thus, currently, our institutional and personal resources are not oriented to assist with it. Finally, any text exploring how death can be a healing event must consider the cultural and spiritual resistance to ending life. Our culture has been shaped by a religious stream that has condemned the intentional ending of life.

And this fifth fact becomes the subject of the second chapter, in which I will examine the Abrahamic religions: Judaism, Christianity, and Islam, and their respective responses to medical assistance in dying. It has been a tradition for over 3,000 years that the belief in an all-powerful Creator has meant that believers would not transgress the final divide and presume to end their lives before their appointed time, as if they were beyond the Creator's control. Recently, some Protestant churches have nuanced this position with pronouncements that would allow for some exceptions, notably abortion and now medical assistance in dying.[19] This chapter will take a closer examination of a position, taken by the United Church of Canada, which promotes itself as a "balanced" position.[20]

Moving from the explicit theological objections to ethical propositions, the third chapter in this book will explore how the advances in medical technology have considerably confounded a neat distinction between living and dying. The argument advanced by some conservative religious traditions that we should not "play God" by ending life prematurely or intentionally, is either unaware of or unwilling to admit the fact that we have long passed the time when God was the singular agent involved in our living and dying. Modern science has pushed the boundaries of life in so many ways that it becomes difficult to determine when, if ever, a divine hand is involved in closing down our living. Moreover, there is considerable doubt when our quality of living is more suitably called a stage of our dying. And the real question becomes at what point, and to what extent, do we help the natural course of dying to take over?

Having advanced the argument over dying to this stage, I will propose in the fourth chapter my central thesis in its complete form. By making a distinction between "curing the disease" and "healing the illness," I will advance the argument that we can "heal" people as they die. Using a personal experience, I will argue that all human beings die of a disease . . . no matter the interventions

---

19. See the position paper published by the United Church of Canada, "United Church Opts."

20. See United Church of Canada, "Medical Assistance in Dying."

of our medical system, eventually one disease or another will win. But the illness, which is the sociological and emotional condition imposed by the disease, can be healed even at the moment of death. Alas, most of our resources in the health system are used in trying to cure the disease, and very few are left over for the very important task of healing the illness.

In chapter five, I will outline the best arguments that favor medical assistance in dying, while in chapter six, I will outline a few general arguments against it. In this latter chapter, I will suggest that medical assistance in dying is a lamentable progression of our society. There is little question that the current legislation gives priority to individual rights over collective values, and that poses problems not simply for the way we shape society, but also has the unintended effect of placing some specific groups within society in a more vulnerable position. Once we have breached the unassailable ultimateness of life and made it a contingent choice, some vulnerable groups are placed in jeopardy. And as we move forward, some attention to this new dynamic is necessary. How do we place limits on the subjectivism that has been legitimized by this legislative change?

Chapter seven offers a few practical suggestions for pastoral care. Gathering the best advice from those who have passed through the process of medical assistance in dying, we can make some initial suggestions about ritual and pragmatic steps that will ease the journey of our ending. We are still so new to this approach to living and dying that we are having to develop an entire vocabulary, practice, and approach, to capture it with both dignity and efficiency. Currently, we are fumbling and clumsy in how we speak and administer medical assistance to help people have a healing death.

I conclude this text with a story that acts as an affirmation about the underlying principle of the Abrahamic tradition, which has always posited a "justice beyond justice," or what some biblical commentators call a higher righteousness.[21] Put simply, there has always been a law of divine compassion and grace that defines all

---

21. See Brown, *Birth of the Messiah*, 73–74.

other laws. In the declaration that God's will is for fullness of life rather than its longevity, practitioners argue that we must allow certain circumstances to grant exceptions to the seventh commandment, taking life. In this regard, I was struck by the clarity of Martine Partridge, a Canadian woman who recently ended her life with assistance and made this step because she cherished life so dearly. Hers wasn't a capitulation to death, but a declaration of living. In a letter to her family and friends she said:

> I choose medical assistance in death because I love and cherish life. For me life is to be lived as Thoreau described: "deliberately. . . . I did not wish to live what was not life, living is so dear. . . . I wanted to live deep and suck out all the marrow of life."[22]

---

22. Martine Partridge, in a letter to her family and friends explaining her decision to seek medical assistance to end her life. *Calgary Sun*, June 16, 2017.

Chapter 1

FIVE FACTS ABOUT MEDICAL ASSISTANCE IN DYING

> Do not go gentle into that good night.
> Rage! Rage against the dying of the light.
> —Dylan Tomas

Introduction[1]

"We shoot horses, don't we?" That's Phyllis, my faithful counsel and chief critic at the church where I serve. And to answer my general question about the appropriateness of medical assistance in dying, she replied with her typical common sense. "Surely we can show mercy to fellow beings who are suffering." End of sermon!

Choosing the time of your own death has always been possible, but until the recent implementation of Bill C-14, it was both

---

1. The basic structure of this introduction was first published in the *United Church Observer* column "Conundrums," November 2017.

FIVE FACTS ABOUT MEDICAL ASSISTANCE IN DYING

illegal and immoral. Stemming from the Abrahamic tradition's aversion to "playing God," we considered that ending one's life was a selfish, presumptive act. How dare we rewrite the providential play book! Our nation's Criminal Code and our common vocabulary reflected that position. You don't *do* suicide, you *commit* it, because, apart from everything else, it's a crime.

But, as Phyllis intuited, everyone will concede that compassion trumps law when someone is declining into intolerable suffering. If you're living with incurable cancer or ALS, for instance, you get a pass. No one should have to go through the indignity and pain that ALS entails. It robs you of your bodily functions, one by one, exacting tremendous pain, as you decline to the point where your only hope is to communicate through eye movement. In a similar fashion, Huntington's or Parkinson's or any variety of cancers and contagions steals pieces of our dignity until we are a shell. We can still love, of course, and be the object of loving. We are able to think and feel, grieve and rejoice—though often no one could tell—and yet at what cost! Eventually, it becomes too much to bear. And people want out of the shame.

"We shoot horses, don't we?" Of course we do. Compassion wins.

And to those who argue we are playing God—trespassing on heaven's prerogative—I would invite us to look carefully into the eyes of those whose lives are being artificially sustained through surgical or medicinal intervention and recognize there is little left of that argument. If there was a divine line in the sand beyond which we, as mortal human beings, should not pass, we left that boundary long ago. The current state of medical science leaves little doubt that we are extending life well beyond natural limits—often to the joy of those who live, sometimes to the dismay of those who would like to die.

And while there is no question that everyone must die, we have achieved a measure of success in postponing the inevitability of death or at least making it more tolerable. The argument of this text is that medical assistance in dying is another tool—as much as chemotherapy might be, for instance, in the treatment of our living into dying.

But before embracing this new regime of medical assistance in dying, there are some background "facts" that will inform our analysis and assist us in our interpretation and implementation of this new procedure.

We begin with the specifics of the recent legislative and personal history that led to the current position, and it is not surprising that ALS is at the heart of the debate.

Fact One: A Specific History

Amyotrophic Lateral Sclerosis[2] (ALS or "Lou Gehrig's disease") is a horrible neurological disorder that begins with minor symptoms of muscle weakness or inability to control voluntary muscle movement and ends with respiratory failure. Its particular horror is that our five senses are largely unaffected through the rapid progression of the disease. And even though most other bodily functions become nonresponsive, one can still sense the world round about. One is literally trapped, fully conscious and cognitive, in a body that does not respond. Unable to speak, many people living with ALS are reduced to communicating through blinking sequences.

The prognosis of ALS is grim. Most people die rapidly, between two and four years after diagnosis, and currently there is no cure or very little medical intervention available to retard the progression of the disease. Professor Stephen Hawking, who lived for over fifty years with ALS, is a unique exception to the norm. While there are great advances in neurological sciences, ALS is still a nightmare.

It was this knowledge that led Sue Rodriguez, a forty-two-year-old mother from Vancouver, Canada, who was diagnosed with ALS in 1992, to seek redress. When she discovered she would not live more than a year, she began a challenge to strike down section 241(b) of the Canadian Criminal Code. That statute made

2. See Appendix for greater detail on ALS as a motor neuron disease.

physician assisted suicide illegal. While it was not an offence for an able-bodied person to end their own life, anyone who was unable to end their life on their own, and who therefore needed help assisting them to do so, would subject these assistants to prosecution. At the time, her appeal went all the way to the Supreme Court of Canada, and in a divided decision, the Court ruled against her. They determined that there was no infringement of her section 7 charter rights to life, liberty, and security of the person. Unable to obtain a legal right to end her life with medical assistance, she later was able to secure relief from an anonymous physician on February 12, 1994, in a controversial event that captured national attention for a time.

It would be almost a decade later that Gloria Taylor, a woman in agony with ALS, and Kay Carter, who suffered from degenerative spinal stenosis (an abnormal narrowing of the spinal canal), launched a new appeal. In what became known as the "Carter" decision,[3] the Supreme Court reversed itself and brought down a unanimous decision. It is remarkable that this ruling was signed "The Court," meaning there was no doubt as to its solid approbation. In order to demonstrate a violation of section 7, any claimant must show that the law infringes on their rights to life, liberty, and security. At this point, the Court determined that while section 217 of the Criminal Code offered protection to the wider population against any arbitrary ending of life, it did "overreach" the principle of natural justice for a select few individuals who might be influenced or indeed forced to take their own life earlier than they might otherwise wish because of their fear that they would be unable to perform the task when their disease had progressed. Further, those who were grievously ill, suffering from irremediable and painful conditions, would have their liberty seriously infringed, because they could not make fundamental decisions about their bodily integrity. Likewise, leaving people like Ms. Taylor to endure intolerable pain infringed on her right to security.

While there are many legal details in this reversal that escape the common citizen, it is reasonable to suggest that, during the

3. Carter was the name of the claimant who made the appeal.

intervening years between Rodriguez and Carter, we have had a shift in our general understanding of individual rights, giving more power to a person to direct their lives free from the interference of the state. In equal measure, we have come to appreciate the concepts of life, liberty, and security in broader terms. Life is not merely the biological functioning of an organism. It is a quality of existence. It might also be the case that as our society grows more secular, it distances itself from precepts of the religious traditions that previously directed, either implicitly or explicitly, its lawmakers.

In the Carter decision, the Court gave the federal Parliament one year (it was later extended by four months) to prepare legislation or amend the Criminal Code to correct the infringements of Charter rights found in the pertinent sections of the Criminal Code dealing with suicide and assistance in dying. The deadline period coincided with a change in government. In December 2015, a parliamentary committee was established to take a report to the government by February 2016, which it did. This committee interviewed over 140 representatives of interest groups, religious organizations, and civil and ethical experts, and produced a report entitled "Medical Assistance in Dying, a Patient-Centered Approach,"[4] which later resulted in Bill C-14.[5]

The committee made several important decisions, which would later find their way into law. First, they determined that this was a medical issue not a legal one. They would, therefore, place the responsibility on physicians for determining categories of informed consent, tolerance for pain and diagnosis of irremediable physical conditions—all of which would factor into offering an individual medical assistance in dying.

The committee also changed the name of this "procedure" from "physician assisted death," which focused on the doctor as the chief agent, to "medical assistance in dying," which placed the

---

4. The full report can be found online. See Ogilvie and Oliphant, "Medical Assistance in Dying."

5. The full text of the bill is found online. See "Bill C-14" in the bibliography as well as the Appendix of this text.

emphasis back on the patient who was requesting and receiving "assistance" with their state of living. This took the issue out of the courts' and the lawyers' hands. It would be up to two doctors to determine the appropriateness of this procedure, in consultation, of course, with a consenting, requesting patient and their families. This illustrates not only the esteem in which we hold medical professionals, it also points to a bias. We would rather place end of life decisions within the context of a conversation at the bedside, rather than the adversarial climate of a court room. A wise presumption.

Through its consultations, the committee determined that they would grant conscientious objection, as had been tested in the courts on issues like abortion, so that no physician or health care provider would be required to offer assistance in dying, if it went contrary to their religious convictions. The stipulation of the report was that those who chose not to extend this assistance to their patient were required to offer "effective referral," so that the individual in question would not be without the care they desired. Institutions, however, have no such conscience, and if any publicly funded institution was asked for assistance in dying, that institution was required to provide it, no matter their religious affiliation.

There were objections raised by the Roman Catholic representatives to this requirement, suggesting that anyone who asked for medical assistance in dying who was in a "Catholic" hospital could sign themselves out, move to a motel nearby and have the procedure. But as will be noted below, such an idea is both unworkable and cruel and obscures the fact that the hospital, in receiving public funding, has made a covenant with the government to carry out any and all legally sanctioned procedures to the best of its ability.

The committee affirmed, and it was later placed within Bill C-14, that if anyone used medical assistance in dying, their cause of death would be listed as the irremediable disease from which they were suffering. This was not to be considered as "suicide," and there would, therefore, be no ramifications with respect to insurance policies or pension benefits.

One final note. The committee placed medical assistance in dying, as the title implies, within a full range of other procedures. It was not the immediate first or final step, but one possibility along with many others on the continuum of palliative and hospice care. This was not a walk-in clinic procedure, but one done within a range of other interventions intended to make dying as wholesome as possible, free from intolerable suffering and within the context of several important checks and balances.

The report of the committee was submitted. Bill C-14 was brought forward, and after some back and forth debate between the House and Senate, it was signed into law on June 17, 2016.

Fact Two: Bill C-14

The public press has adopted the acronym "M.A.I.D."[6] for "Medical Assistance in Dying," and while many Canadians know of the idea, fewer are aware of the actual stipulations and criteria involved in accessing this relatively new procedure. In some instances, we imagine that it will resolve the nightmare scenario we all fear: a prolonged, vegetable-like state in which our end of life is reduced to intolerable indignity. In recent years, our common dread focuses on Alzheimer's disease, a condition that robs us of self-awareness and personal identity, while leaving a biologically functioning body. Alas, this law does nothing to assuage these apprehensions. As with other civil codes, like licensing regulations for driving at an advanced age, it behooves every citizen to understand clearly what this new law can and cannot do.

There are three sections of the Act that give the basic parameters within which to understand this new medical possibility: Eligibility, Safeguards, and Independent Witnesses.

According to the Act, a person may receive medical assistance in dying if they meet five basic criteria:

---

6. You will note that I have resisted using this acronym since it has a pejorative connotation of "service" and because we are still in our infancy in developing vocabulary around medical assistance in dying, which gives it the dignity and *gravitas* that it deserves.

FIVE FACTS ABOUT MEDICAL ASSISTANCE IN DYING

1. they are eligible—or, but for any applicable minimum period of residence or waiting period, would be eligible—for health services funded by a government in Canada;

2. they are at least 18 years of age and capable of making decisions with respect to their health;

3. they have a grievous and irremediable medical condition;

4. they have made a voluntary request for medical assistance in dying that, in particular, was not made as a result of external pressure; and

5. they give informed consent to receive medical assistance in dying after having been informed of the means that are available to relieve their suffering, including palliative care.[7]

And while the age of majority may seem arbitrary, it has not been the subject of either concerted legal challenge or public debate.[8] In contrast, there is considerable debate about what represents a grievous and "irremediable medical condition." To clarify the legal position, the Act further stipulates that:

> A person has a grievous and irremediable medical condition only if they meet all of the following criteria:
> a) they have a serious and incurable illness, disease, or disability;
> b) they are in an advanced state of irreversible decline in capability;
> c) that illness, disease, or disability or that state of decline causes them enduring physical or psychological suffering that is intolerable to them and that cannot be relieved under conditions that they consider acceptable; and
> d) their natural death has become reasonably foreseeable, taking into account all of their medical circumstances, without a prognosis necessarily having

---

7. Taken directly from the text of the Act . . . see the Appendix.
8. There is currently a parliamentary reexamination of this age-restriction condition within the law, as was anticipated by the initial report.

been made as to the specific length of time that they have remaining.

The first three of these definitions have both objective and subjective elements. A disease, its symptoms, and resultant pain levels are discernable and verifiable. The level of intolerable pain is more personal. Each disease manifests itself differently in each patient, and so the level of "tolerability" may also vary widely. Nevertheless, the law allows considerable leeway in the interpretation of these factors. What is insufferable for one may be acceptable for another.

What is at issue in the press and courts is the fourth stipulation—that death must be "reasonably foreseeable." While almost all the other jurisdictions who allow medical assistance in dying have something similar to this criterion for allowing someone to get help in ending their life, this was not part of the Carter decision, and it may well be subject to a further Carter challenge.[9] The argument for retaining some reference to a "terminal" disease or "foreseeable" end is to protect those at risk with either physiological disorders or non-life threatening illnesses. This may seem to be a small point, but there is implicit within the current law an assumption that this procedure is part of the treatment for unendurable dying and not a relief from intolerable living. The former focuses on making death a dignified, if not a healing, event,[10] while the latter implies something closer to assisted suicide.

The Supreme Court gave its judgment that such a new approach to dying was possible within a modern society, as long as there were "robust" measures in place to protect against either arbitrary or unintentionally coercive pressures placed on those who were most vulnerable in our society: those with debilitating disorders or those with pre-existing physical or psychological conditions. In response, the Act offers the following safeguards: Before a medical practitioner or nurse practitioner provides a person

---

9. At the time of writing, just such a challenge is being mounted by a seventy-seven-year-old woman whose death may or may not be "reasonable foreseeable." See Hasham, "77-Year-Old."

10. This will we be taken up in greater detail in chapters 3 and 4.

with medical assistance in dying, the medical practitioner or nurse practitioner must

- a) be of the opinion that the person meets all of the criteria set out in subsection (1);
- b) ensure that the person's request for medical assistance in dying was
    - (i) made in writing and signed and dated by the person or by another person under subsection (4), and
    - (ii) signed and dated after the person was informed by a medical practitioner or nurse practitioner that the person has a grievous and irremediable medical condition;
- c) be satisfied that the request was signed and dated by the person—or by another person under subsection(4)—before two independent witnesses who then also signed and dated the request;
- d) ensure that the person has been informed that they may, at any time and in any manner, withdraw their request;
- e) ensure that another medical practitioner or nurse practitioner has provided a written opinion confirming that the person meets all of the criteria set out in subsection(1);
- f) be satisfied that they and the other medical practitioner or nurse practitioner referred to in paragraph (e) are independent;
- g) ensure that there are at least 10 clear days between the day on which the request was signed by or on behalf of the person and the day on which the medical assistance in dying is provided or—if they and the other medical practitioner or nurse practitioner referred to in paragraph (e) are both of the opinion that the person's death, or the loss of their capacity to provide informed consent, is imminent—any shorter period that the first medical practitioner or nurse practitioner considers appropriate in the circumstances;

    h) immediately before providing the medical assistance in dying, give the person an opportunity to withdraw their request and ensure that the person gives express consent to receive medical assistance in dying; and

    i) if the person has difficulty communicating, take all necessary measures to provide a reliable means by which the person may understand the information that is provided to them and communicate their decision.

These stipulations are designed to ensure that no one is inadvertently or impetuously caught by a decision they might regret or not understand. The ten-day waiting period allows for a serious regret or re-consideration of a previous decision, and while that seems reasonable, there are some concerns with regard to the eighth stipulation: that immediately before providing medical assistance in dying a person's continued express consent should be obtained. It may well force some who have declined into an unconscious state (either through natural causes or medical intervention) to be aroused back into consciousness and therefore into the uncontrollable pain from which they sought relief in order to give that final confirmation of their intentions. There is considerable doubt whether someone who is thus re-subjected to suffering is capable of rational or consistently reliable thought. In this case, what looks on the surface like a reasonable verification of intent may actually result in cruel and unusual punishment.[11] And as will be noted in chapter 6 of this book, the actual application of these safeguards is still cumbersome and inconsistent across the country.

Fact Three: The Medical Momentum to Cure Disease

During the debate in the United Church over the ordination of self-declared homosexual persons, I recall a story of one gay

---

11. It was based on this prospect that the co-chair of the committee that produced the report which led to the legislation, the Reverend Robert Oliphant, eventually voted against the Bill when it was brought forward.

FIVE FACTS ABOUT MEDICAL ASSISTANCE IN DYING

minister who went home to speak to his mother about his position in favor of eliminating any restrictions to ministry based on sexual orientation. She was adamant in her opposition. She laid down her position clearly, "I don't know any gay ministers." Her son replied with the simple truth, "Yes, you do, Mom." And her reply became a statement of the church's double standard on the issue, "Yes, I know, but I don't want to know that I know." There is a new order of consciousness, when what we know in private is made public and we have to acknowledge it as a fact.

There is a similar dynamic taking place within the medical profession as we start to implement medical assistance in dying. In the past, there has been an unspoken practice of offering enough medication so that those who are enduring insufferably are "comfortable." Of course, no one would admit openly that these patients might be overdosing on morphine or some other barbiturate. All the caregivers knew what they were doing, but they didn't want it made public. The system did not want to know that it knew.

And while this may seem a bit duplicitous, the simple fact is our medical system is not oriented toward tolerating, or in any way acquiescing in, the face of death. From the time students enter medical school, nursing programs, or health care courses, the priority is to save life or at the least "do no harm." Compassion and care are primary. How does the Hippocratic Oath put it?

> I will use treatment to help the sick according to my ability and judgment, but never with a view to injury and wrong-doing. Neither will I administer a poison to anybody when asked to do so, nor will I suggest such a course.[12]

It's explicit. Stemming from this ancient code and following through centuries of modern practice, the basic approach "to do no harm" has been the touchstone of medical practice. Helping someone end their life (using poison and, by extension, other

---

12. For Greek original, English translation, and commentary see "Hippocratic Oath."

means) runs contrary to this momentum of compassion. Is there any doubt why some doctors have resisted this new procedure?

Fact Four: The Novelty of Medical Assistance in Dying

It is now two years since Bill C-14 was given Royal Assent, but there is still considerable confusion and apprehension regarding its details. At first it was a novelty . . . something that happened to other people. But with the passing of months, the novelty became a reality and then a realistic option among many that can be considered at the end of life.

And while the actual procedure may now find a more comfortable home among Canadians, the process is still very fresh, encumbered by some of the legal stipulations set in place to guard against abuse. So, for instance, one interviewee argued that those who wish to have medical assistance in dying are required to give consent, not simply at the beginning of discussion with medical experts, but also immediately before the procedure to end life is undertaken.[13] In real terms, this means that those who are suffering from "enduring physical or psychological suffering" and who have been heavily medicated as a consequence, must be "wakened" from this pain-free state to give their final consent. Hence, the legal framework requires some to suffer again the pain for which the procedure was a remedy.

For others, the request for medical assistance in dying was met by confused or fumbling administrators who didn't even have the vocabulary, let alone the protocols, to ensure that the help they had to offer was, indeed, just that and not a furtherance of unnecessary hardship.[14]

---

13. See footnote 11 above. This inadvertent but quite concrete cruelty was one of the main reasons why the co-chair of the parliamentary committee, Robert Oliphant, declined to vote in favor of the Bill when it was finally presented.

14. See the news story concerning Jan Lackie's father, who was shifted from one hospital to another to receive medical assistance in dying and who went

And the challenges of medical assistance in dying go further than confusing or contradictory procedures. The wider society has not yet understood how it differs from euthanasia, how it is and is not a solution to the emotional turmoil that grips both the dying and those who walk with them through the dark valley. While it remains one of a number of procedures, much like other advances in medical skill, medical assistance in dying has yet to be understood as a tool for healing death.

Fact Five: Shifting Away from Spiritual Resistance

This sluggish appraisal of medical assistance in dying is made complicated by the historical resistance of the Abrahamic religions to suicide. And given that medical assistance in dying is both communal and consensual, it still seems to abrogate the principle of divine providence. The God who holds life and death is set aside as humans take dying into their own hands. Can we really play that game without falling into the trap of pride? Do human beings have the wisdom to weigh such choices? In Charles Dickens' *A Christmas Carol*, the Ghost of Christmas Present warns Scrooge, who had argued that some people should die in order to decrease the surplus population:

> "Man," said the Ghost, "if man you be in heart, not adamant, forbear that wicked cant until you have discovered What the surplus is, and Where it is. Will you decide what men shall live, what men shall die? It may be, that in the sight of Heaven, you are more worthless and less fit to live than millions like this poor man's child. Oh God! To hear the Insect on the leaf pronouncing on the too much life among his hungry brothers in the dust."[15]

And despite religious resistance, most people of common sense recognize that innocent suffering is untenable. Somehow

---

through incredible pain at the very last because of administrative incompetence. See Adach, "'I Can Still Clearly'"; or Blackwell, "B.C. Man."

15. Dickens, *Christas Carol*, 4.

there should be relief offered to those who do not merit agony. "We shoot horses, don't we?"

And as secular society embraces medical assistance in dying, the sensitive among us recognize that it changes us as a community. What was once beyond individual choice has now become possibility, and there is a sense in which we have capitulated to liberal individualism. The line between life and death was rigid, never to be crossed, for it ensured that people in society enjoyed the right to life, no matter what that life might entail. Those in the differently abled community are quick to point out that one of the basic tenets of our society was that no one had to argue for the basic right to the fullness of living. And having crossed this line, we are set adrift. On what basis do we deny an individual's wish and ambition?

One can feel the strains of the shifting legal and theological positions that medical assistance in dying inspires. Almost all the interviews I conducted began with disclaimers about bending religiously held convictions because of the need to alleviate suffering. And it is to explore our deeply held religious convictions that we now turn.

Chapter 2

OUR SPIRITUAL HERITAGE

> ...but when any is taken with a torturing and lingering pain, so that there is no hope, either of recovery or ease, the priests and magistrates come and exhort them, that since they are now unable to go on with the business of life, are become a burden to themselves and to all about them, and they have really outlived themselves, they should no longer nourish such a rooted distemper, but choose rather to die, since they cannot live but in much misery.[1]
>
> —Thomas More

Introduction

David was my age, an avid reader and keen learner.[2] He'd passed many of the same milestones in his life as I had: an accomplished practitioner, respected father, reliable and loving husband, and a playful and trustworthy member of the wider

---

1. Cayley, ed., *Memoirs*, 102–3.
2. Names and circumstances have been altered slightly to ensure anonymity.

community. We enjoyed the odd game of racquetball . . . he had a wicked backhand. And whenever there was a church-based, theological seminar, he was the first to register. I have met few with the same intellectual power and dry sense of humor. Did I mention he played a mean saxophone? At the prime of his life, with no money issues and no obvious distractions or pressures, he declined into despair and eventually took his own life on a bleak winter night. It was clear something was wrong, and while family members tried to reach him, it was to no avail.

For those of us outside the immediate circle, his suicide came as a surprise and a deeply disquieting sorrow. Had we not done enough? Were we so blind to his pain that he walked a lonely path to his own end, not feeling he had anywhere to turn for sympathy and support? How is it possible for someone in our midst to know such a depth of suffering that they feel there is no choice? Clearly, David felt that living was so fraught with broken feelings that it was less agonizing to leave this life than to stay and fight to restore it. What anguish! How did we miss it?

As days passed, apart from the waves of guilt and recrimination, currents of anger and frustration started to emerge. How could he do this to the family? Of course, his wife was beside herself, wounded by sorrow, and behind that pain there was a considerable sense of betrayal. And the kids? There are four children, all now on their own career paths. They were cut adrift. The youngest one was more fragile than a parent might want, and who can tell if her father's untimely death will unhinge all the progress she has made thus far. It had been difficult enough to settle on her dreams, and now who knows if she can hold to the course that she and father had plotted out.

The extended family was devastated by the loss, of course. They saw David's passing as a travesty—a life cut off too quickly and too soon. Now they would have to pick up added responsibility for David's family, guiding children and grandchildren through the minefield of doubts and dismay that the suicide of a parent can create.

When we are young, suicide is *the* great temptation. Like looking over the edge of a deep precipice, it has a mysterious, intensely alluring attraction. And who knows if one can hold onto sanity and not jump. When we are young, not having the awareness of the rhythms of living and not appreciating the interplay between light and dark, today and tomorrow, we believe this moment is all we have. If it is filled with pain, we might seek to flee it and act impulsively. These deaths are indeed tragic, because we know, given time and sufficient sympathy, these suicidal temptations pass.

In contrast, the suicide of a mature adult complicates these distressing emotions by an added statement of worthlessness. Having seen much of what this world has to offer, they lose faith and turn it down. It's not as if they don't know and haven't earned some wisdom. They've seen life for what it is, and they're not interested. Who would not feel that our community, its support systems and principles, have been judged and found wanting?

As we turn to the question of the spiritual resistance to ending one's life, it is important to recognize that our arguments have grown from the context of real people taking their own lives. Not theoretical, these questions touch the heart of human hopes and fears. Ending one's life is a very real and very painful reality.

So, as I explore the Abrahamic opposition to suicide and by extension to premature death, I keep David's life and love in my mind. He would be the first to insist on careful and consistent reasoning. I owe him that much.

Judaism: "The Lord Giveth and the Lord Taketh Away" (Job 1:21)

As is the case with many modern social dilemmas, the Bible does not offer direct reference to the question of suicide or medical assistance in dying. The scriptures have eleven instances when suicide took place. Ten are self-inflicted (in two of these examples, the suicide took place after the person in question had been denied in their request to be killed by someone else). Usually taking place within the context of palace intrigues or defeat in battle, ten of the suicides are stories of a "noble" death. The eleventh, the case of Abimelech (Judg 9:52–54), features the only example of "assisted suicide" in scripture. He died because of the action of an armor bearer whom he pleaded to take his life in order to preserve his memory. Being mortally wounded by a woman, Abimelech beseeched: "Draw your sword and kill me, so people will not say about me, 'A woman killed him.'" While there are quite an array of "suicides"[3] in Jewish tradition, this final one is not so flattering, but

---

3. 1) *Judg 16:30*—"Then Samson said, 'Let me die with the Philistines.' He strained with all his might; and the house fell on the lords and all the people who were in it. So those he killed at his death were more than those he had killed during his life." 2) *1 Sam 31:4*—"Then Saul said to his armor-bearer, 'Draw your sword and thrust me through with it, so that these uncircumcised may not come and thrust me through, and make sport of me.' But his armor-bearer was unwilling; for he was terrified. So Saul took his own sword and fell upon it." 3) *1 Sam 31:5*—"When his armor-bearer saw that Saul was dead, he also fell upon his sword and died with him." 4) *2 Sam 17:23*—"When Ahithophel saw that his counsel was not followed, he saddled his donkey and went off home to his own city. He set his house in order, and hanged himself; he died and was buried in the tomb of his father." 5) *1 Kgs 16:18*—"When Zimri saw that the city was taken, he went into the citadel of the king's house; he burned down the king's house over himself with fire, and died." 6) *1 Chr 10:4*—"Then Saul said to his armor-bearer, 'Draw your sword, and thrust me through with it, so that these uncircumcised may not come and make sport of me.' But his armor-bearer was unwilling, for he was terrified. So Saul took his own sword and fell on it." 7) (Apocrypha) *1 Macc 6:46*—"He got under the elephant, stabbed it from beneath, and killed it; but it fell to the ground upon him and he died." 8) (Apocrypha) *2 Macc 10:12*—"Ptolemy, who was called Macron, took the lead in showing justice to the Jews because of the wrong that had been done to them, and attempted to maintain peaceful relations with them." 9) (Apocrypha) *2 Macc 14:41*—"When the troops were about to capture the tower and were forcing the door of the courtyard, they ordered that fire be brought and the doors burned. Being surrounded, Razis fell upon his own sword." 10) *Matt 27:5*—"Throwing down the pieces of silver in the temple, [Judas] departed; and he went and hanged himself." 11) *Judg 9:52-4*—"Abimelech came to the tower, and fought against it, and came near to the entrance of the tower to burn it with fire. But a certain woman threw an upper millstone on Abimelech's head, and crushed his skull. Immediately he called to the young man who carried his armour and said to him, 'Draw your sword and kill me, so people will not say about me, "A woman killed him."' So the young man thrust him through, and he died."

is clearly "assisted suicide." Again, no commentary is offered either in favour or opposition to Abimelech's last request.

It is noteworthy to realize that in none of these eleven examples was the suicide called "sinful." Indeed, in all cases there is no commentary at all. It happened. Present indicative; no emotional adverbial phrases or painful adjectives. Furthermore, in every instance the question of unbearable physical anguish was never considered. Indeed, the suicides were all a matter of political or social expediency. One can assume, in at least one instance—the suicide of Judas in Matthew's gospel (27:5)—that the audience would have received the news with satisfaction. His suicide was a just, fitting end for a traitor. In contrast, there is little doubt that the first suicide in the biblical story (Judg 16:30), that of Sampson pulling the temple down upon himself, would have been retold with pride, for his suicide was both courageous and patriotic. One could easily see his ending as a testament to faith and trust in God—following the divine will even unto death.

There are four other stories in which the question of suicide is explicitly mentioned: two involve a prophet, one is found in Job and a final example is in part of a letter from the Apostle Paul.[4] Let us hold this last example until we explore the Christian attitudes to suicide. It then becomes important to separate our analysis of the motivations behind these other suicidal musings into two groups: the prophets and Job. In this way, we will outline the chief objections to suicide raised within the Jewish faith tradition.

---

4. 1) *Jonah 4:8*—"When the sun rose, God prepared a sultry east wind, and the sun beat down on the head of Jonah so that he was faint and asked that he might die. He said, 'It is better for me to die than to live.'" 2) *Job 6:8-9*—"'O that I might have my request, and that God would grant my desire; that it would please God to crush me, that he would let loose his hand and cut me off!'" 3) *Elijah in 1 Kgs 19:4*—"But he himself went a day's journey into the wilderness, and came and sat down under a solitary broom tree. He asked that he might die: 'It is enough; now, O LORD, take away my life, for I am no better than my ancestors.'" 4) *Phil 1:21-24*—"For to me, living is Christ and dying is gain. If I am to live in the flesh, that means fruitful labor for me; and I do not know which I prefer. I am hard pressed between the two: my desire is to depart and be with Christ, for that is far better; but to remain in the flesh is more necessary for you."

Almost every young child knows the story of the prophet Jonah, how he tried to evade his destiny and God's explicit commands to preach repentance to the town of Nineveh whose wickedness was repugnant to the Almighty. Instead of following this clear directive, Jonah takes passage on a ship destined for Tarshish . . . the other direction from God's command. A storm rises and the sailors, after casting lots, inquire of Jonah what he has done, and when the prophet confesses that he is "fleeing from the presence of the Lord" (Jonah 1:10b), it is agreed that he should be cast into the sea, and that is when he is swallowed by a "big fish" (whales are part of the later elaboration of the story). In the belly of this sea beast, Jonah repents and commits himself to follow God's commands and is consequently vomited out by the fish onto the land close to Nineveh.

Following God's original plan, Jonah prophecies against Nineveh's injustices and wickedness. Giving the people forty days to clean up their act, Jonah waits for the anger of the Lord to be visited upon this evil city. Contrary to his expectations, the King and then the people repent of their sins. They put on sackcloth and cover themselves with ash—even the domestic animals are thus marked by signs of remorse and repentance. The people turn to God, and God "repented of the evil he had said he would do to them" (Jonah 3:10). Dodged that bullet.

Instead of being relieved, Jonah is angry. This was not what he expected. Surely these foreigners deserved to be punished, and instead God has shown mercy. After all his ordeals, Jonah felt either betrayed or belittled or both and asks that God take his life. This then ensures a dialogue. Actually, it's an object lesson with God, in which his Creator tries to show Jonah that he is not in charge of the earth's cycles of life and death. Nonplused, Jonah insists again, "It is better for me to die than to live" (Jonah 4:8b). He appears more like a spoiled child than a principled prophet.

Apart from the important lesson of recalling that it is God who is ruler of heaven and earth, the prophet Jonah is an object lesson in suicide. You are not allowed to end your life because you didn't get what you want. No escaping this existence when things don't go your way. That's not an option. Whether it's a question of your personal disappointments or a broken heart, life is a gift given by God. To obey God is to live—through shadow as well as light—for the goodness of creation contains both day and night. Faithfulness requires that we not escape this life out of petulance, despair, or egotism.

The second prophet story of suicide is a similar example of trying to snatch defeat out of the jaws of victory. Elijah has returned to the wilderness, having thoroughly defeated the 450 prophets of Baal on Mount Carmel. They tried to make it rain through invocations to their false God, but the Maker of Heaven and Earth favored Elijah, and having accepted his sacrifice, sent rain down upon the parched land. The people consequently repented and turned to God. The prophets of Baal were killed by the people, and being pursued by the enraged agents of Jezebel, Elijah heads off into the desert. He's had it. Exhausted and tired of being beaten by the forces of evil, he wants to die: "It is enough; now, O Lord, take away my life, for I am no better than my ancestors" (1 Kgs 194b).

In this case, the prophet is not acting out of a churlish attitude, feeling snubbed or betrayed. On the contrary, Elijah is tired of being right. It's been overwhelming to have the weight of the people's salvation on his shoulders, and he now wants a pass. By extension, you could argue that Elijah represents the elder who feels they have accomplished all that there is to their life's vocation. He was afraid he couldn't meet the next challenge. And the obvious implication of the Elijah story is that it is God who decides when life is complete. Who knows what miracles God has in store for us, even when we think we have arrived at the end of our energies.

In both these examples, the underlying principle is that God holds all life. It does not belong to any individual, no matter how successful or noble they might think themselves to be. To be blunt: life is not a possession—like a house or book. We are stewards of the earth, including our own lives. This means we live with the dialectic of being principally responsible for, but not ultimately in charge of, our existence.⁵ God reserves the right to end life, and our role is to accept in faith and trust that God knows better than we do ourselves what our life represents. To short-circuit God's plan by taking our own life is to deny the amazing grace that holds each of us.

In the case of Jonah, the motivation for suicide was self-serving disappointment, and with Elijah it was exhaustion and fear of his own fallibility. In either case, ending your own life is not an option.

The book of Job raises yet another reason to end life: unendurable suffering. Containing perhaps the greatest poem in the biblical record, the book of Job is known to everyone in some way or another, for we all suffer disease and distress. In Job's case, he is the victim of a seemingly silly divine bet between Yahweh and the devil (hardly complimentary of God). They are wagering over Job's faithfulness. Since his life had been blessed, the devil speculated he would renounce his faith if his fortunes were reversed. To prove his side of the bet, God does just that. He visits Job with horrendous misery, the loss of his children, his cattle, his vast fortune, and finally his personal health. He is covered with sores from the tip of his head to his feet and is in constant distress. Job's state is so miserable that he uses an old pot to scrape his scabs, as he sits amid ashes: the portrait of repentance and God-abandonment. Having no faith in God, Job's wife sees his anguish and suggests suicide, "Curse God and die" (Job 2:9b).

The principle point of the book of Job is to refute the traditional theological formula that if you do good you will be blessed, and that if your life shows signs of distress, it is evidence that you have sinned in some way. There's no *quid pro quo* in heaven's judgement. This is certainly a departure from other texts, especially the Psalms, which argue precisely that the good are favored while the evil are destroyed.⁶ In the context of this debate, it becomes obvious that Job's faith is his salvation, and despite his maladies and

---

5. For a more thorough examination of this dialectic there is no better book than *The Steward*, written by John Douglas Hall.

6. See Pss 1, 3, 14, 107.

the misguided counsels of his wife and friends, he will not give up on God or seek an easy way out. According to his first "comforter," who tries to make Job see that he must have done something to deserve his dismal state, if only he would repent and admit his errors, all would be well. But it is never that simple. Job is steadfast in his belief he has done nothing wrong or unrighteous. To make his point, he even invites God to end his life: "O that I might have my request, and that God would grant my desire; that it would please God to crush me, that he would let loose his hand and cut me off!" (Job 6:8–9). Laying his life at God's feet, Job invites God to do whatever is right.

This pronouncement is in continuity with his first faithful pronouncement when his affliction began. Job pronounces his absolute trust in God, in words that have since become the touchstone of Jewish thought: "the Lord giveth and the Lord taketh away. Blessed be the name of the Lord" (Job 1:21). And this must be the chief principle that condemns or seriously discourages suicide. It is not the sixth commandment against killing but the general principle that we do not usurp God's role in creating and extinguishing life.[7] To do so is to breach the first commandment, to place yourself and your personal desires above God. Moreover, it acts as the ultimate denunciation of trust and faith.

Therefore, those who end their lives in full and conscious awareness of what they are doing are, according to the Talmud, to be denied rituals and rights accorded to the righteous who die.[8]

---

7. The sixth commandment is often translated "thou shalt not kill" (Exod 20:13). In the Hebrew Torah, the verb "ratsah," which translates more as "murder" than "kill" and refers to the criminal act of killing a human being, is used. The neutral verb for "to kill" in Hebrew is "harag." One might therefore translate this commandment, as is the case in the New Revised Standard Version, as "You shall not murder." This would imply that the injunction is against taking life for heinous reasons and against the express desires of the victim. In that case, it would have little to say to the issue of medical assistance in dying, in which the "victim" is actually asking to end their life and in a way that is not unanticipated or cruel, but consciously and freely.

8. "Suicide in Jewish law is a very serious offense. The Talmud says, 'For him who takes his own life with full knowledge of his action [the Hebrew word is b'daat] no rites are to be observed. . . . There is to be no rending of clothes and

There are instances when an exception can be made. If someone is not in full possession of their faculties or suffering some form of compulsion,[9] exceptions can be granted as one might argue was the case of King Saul, who knew he would be ill-treated or tortured if he were captured. The same could be said for the mass suicides at the end of the siege of Masada.

And given that Jesus spoke out of the Jewish context of his time, there is little question that he also adhered to the same positions on suicide as I have outlined above. There is no need to make stark distinctions between Christian ethical perspectives on taking one's life and those outlined in Judaism.

Christianity: "Love Your Neighbor as Yourself"

If there is an explicit Christian resistance to suicide, we might center it in a phrase taken from Leviticus[10] that is used in the telling of the story of the Good Samaritan (Luke 10:25–37). The lawyer, who seeks to defend his righteousness by telling Jesus that he has kept the statues of the Torah, quotes Deuteronomy proclaiming that the chief commandment is to love the Lord God with heart

---

no eulogy. But people should line up for him [at the end of the burial ceremony] and the mourner's blessing should be recited [as the family passes through] out of respect for the living. The general rule is: Whatever rites are [normally] performed for the benefit of the survivors should be observed; whatever is [normally] done out of respect for the dead should not be observed'" (See "Issues in Jewish Ethics").

9. "Jewish law does not, however, place all suicides in the same category. One category of suicide, as stated above, includes those who are in full possession of their physical and mental facilities (*b'daat*) when they take their lives. A second category includes those who act on impulse or who are under severe mental strain or physical pain when committing suicide. Jewish law speaks of an individual in this second category of being "an *anuss*, meaning a 'person under compulsion,' and hence not responsible for his actions. All burial and mourning rites are observed for him" (See "Issues in Jewish Ethics").

10. Lev 19:18: "You shall not take vengeance or bear a grudge against the sons of your own people, but you shall love your neighbor as yourself: I am the Lord."

and soul, mind and strength,[11] and then he adds another most famous passage from Leviticus: "and you shall love your neighbor as yourself." It is at that point that Jesus tells his most famous parable, and the point is surely to expand the concept of neighbor. In Leviticus, there is an implicit assumption that one's neighbors are part of the close circle of friends within Judaism. What Jesus intends is to expand that concept of neighbor to include even the enemy, in this case the heretic Samaritans. We're no longer talking about just respecting and forgiving our extended family, we have to do the same for those whom we detest.

A secondary lesson drawn from Jesus' use of Leviticus is that self-love is both expected and necessary. It is the ethical guide and moral measure. Your self-love is a template for loving those beyond your comfort zone.

As with other concepts within scripture, the concept of self-love is much more than an emotional reaction. Of course, we delight and treasure our own life, but we also treat it with the respect and justice we share in all relationships. Our life, being a gift of God, is a sacred trust. Our own life, at God's bequest, is not to be used to destroy beauty or right relationships or just practice. You love your own life by "doing justice, loving mercy and walking humbly with the One who made us."[12]

Therefore, to end one's life is not just a denial of God's gift, it is a betrayal of the self-love by which we are to guide our human community. And while this may not make much difference to the one who has suicided, it changes how we see the community that is left behind. As mentioned above, our attitude to dying speaks volumes about our attitude to living. And in this case, we can appreciate how taking our own life undermines the value with which we hold our life. And by extension, granting the right to an individual to take their own life corrodes the society's ability to embrace the immutable principle of sanctity of life.

There is a second "Christian" response to ending one's life, and it is found in a comment about leaving this world, made by

---

11. Deut 6:4.
12. Mic 6:8.

the Apostle Paul. Of course, Paul is also a Jew speaking out of his devotion to Judaism, but he adds a new aspect to our Abrahamic resistance to suicide. His explicit reference text that pertains to a desire to end one's life is found in his letter to the Philippians. After a traditional greeting and explanation of how the Philippian community is cause for Paul to rejoice (alas, he is more often praying for church communities than rejoicing in them, if we consider his letters to the church in Corinth and Galatia as any indication), he begins to elaborate on his labors in the mission of his community. Then he admits that he is torn between this life and the next. What a choice: to stay and work for the renewal of his communities of faith or to leave this strife-filled world behind and live in eternity with Jesus:

> For to me, living is Christ and dying is gain. If I am to live in the flesh, that means fruitful labor for me; and I do not know which I prefer. I am hard pressed between the two: my desire is to depart and be with Christ, for that is far better; but to remain in the flesh is more necessary for you. (Phil 1:21–24)

The simple point: suicide disrupts the community that is left behind. Our life is not always about us. That sounds counterintuitive, but I am often struck by those who tell me they no longer attend church events because they "don't get anything out of them." "It does nothing for me!" And I would like to respond that "it's not always about you!" We are part of the circle of loving and believing, and it is not simply a question of our own benefit, but also what we might represent or give to others. Human life is actually an interconnectivity of living, and who can guess what my life might mean for others. Certainly, not me! Therefore, to end one's life is to deny the community. As Paul puts it, he stays in this world because "it is necessary" for others.

I have made these Christian arguments against suicide in the context of the biblical references, but St. Augustine and Thomas Aquinas later put the arguments against taking one's own life into the theological tradition in a succinct manner. Aquinas outlines his objections as threefold: the denial of God's will, the betrayal of self-love and the disruption of the community's health.[13] And this has been the backbone of a position that became more institutionalized and strict within the Middle Ages when anyone who suicided was denied the benefits and rituals of a regular funeral and deemed to be condemned to eternal punishment.

It is, therefore, surprising that we find a single exception to the momentum of condemnation surrounding ending one's life. It is found in the book *Utopia*, in which Thomas More, the murdered Lord Chancellor under Henry VIII, spoke of how, in a perfect society, those who were suffering unbearably would be given the chance to end their lives with dignity:

> I have already told you with what care they look after their sick, so that nothing is left undone that can contribute either to their ease or health: and for those who are taken with fixed and incurable diseases, they use all possible ways to cherish them, and to make their lives as comfortable as possible. They visit them often, and take great pains to make their time pass off easily: but when any is taken with a torturing and lingering pain, so that there is no hope, either of recovery or ease, the priests and magistrates come and exhort them, that since they are now unable to go on with the business of life, are become a burden to themselves and to all about them, and they have really outlived themselves, they should no longer nourish such a rooted distemper, but choose rather to die, since they cannot live but in much misery: being assured, that if they thus deliver themselves from torture, or are willing that others should do it, they shall be happy after death. Since by their acting thus, they lose none of the pleasures but only the troubles of life, they think they behave not only reasonably, but in a manner consistent with religion and piety; because they follow the advice given them by their priests, who are the expounders of the will of God. Such as are wrought on by these persuasions, either starve themselves of their own accord, or take opium, and by that means die without pain. But no man is forced on this way of ending his life; and if they

---

13. Aquinas, *Summa Theologiae*, 2a2ae, question 64, article 5.

cannot be persuaded to it, this does not induce them to fail in their attendance and care of them; but as they believe that a voluntary death, when it is chosen upon such an authority, is very honorable.[14]

Perhaps More comes closest to the modern debate in which suicide or taking one's own life is not to deny the gift of God, but to fulfill it with honesty and dignity. By his reasoning, suicide does not disrupt the community; instead it gives the collective whole a reverence for right living.

To be fair, More is an exception. Both Protestant and Catholic thinkers side with Aquinas. In the midst of the denials of suicide put forward by Christian theologians—as an act of violence against the complexity of community life—stands an exception: justifiable war theory. Sometimes known as "just war,"[15] this line of reasoning suggests that the taking of life is sometimes justifiable if the threat to the general peace is such that it can only be resisted by violence, potentially deadly violence. The basic point is that the community's safety and security can be sustained only through the use of violence. By extension, it could be argued that suicide is acceptable, if not necessary, in certain special circumstances where a sacrificial act might secure the greater good. And while few would argue with this thinking, and even though the theory is bound by many objective standards and practical applications, it is still bound by subjective judgements that are often as not bound by both selfish and altruistic motivations.

Islam: "And Do Not Throw Yourselves in Destruction"

The third tradition within the Abrahamic family of religions, Islam, follows in the same vein as Judaism and Christianity: seeing

14. More, *Utopia*, Book 2, and quoted at Cayley, ed., *Memoirs*, 102–3. http://www.dignitas.ch/index.php?option=com_content&view=article&id=34&Itemid=74&lang=en.

15. For an extensive review of the theory and its detractors see Yoder, *When War Is Unjust*.

life as a sacred gift from God, and its ending by suicide a direct affront to the power and prerogative of Allah. As is written in the Qur'an:[16]

> It is He who giveth life and who taketh it and to Him shall ye all be brought back. (10:56)

It is clearly stated that God has given each person the gift of life, and as such, it is sacred and to take one's life is to disrespect Allah.[17] As a gift, your life is not your own to do with as you wish.

Unlike the Jewish and Christian sacred writings, suicide is strictly forbidden along with the killing of innocents in Islam, for God is the author of life, and it is only He who could take life.

Of the many verses that forbid suicide, here are the most explicit:

> But let there be amongst you Traffic and trade by mutual good-will: Nor kill (or destroy) yourselves: for verily God hath been to you Most Merciful! If any do that in rancor and injustice, soon shall We cast them into the Fire: And easy it is for God. (Qur'an 4:29–30)

> And do not throw yourselves in destruction. (2:195)

Within Islam, suicide and the penalty for taking one's own life is explicitly outlined:

> If a man kills a believer intentionally, his recompense is Hell, to abide therein (Forever): And the wrath and the curse of God are upon him, and a dreadful penalty is prepared for him. (4:93)

> If any one slew a person—unless it be for murder or for spreading mischief in the land—it would be as if he slew

---

16. Abdul-Khaaliq, "Suicide and Islam."

17. Say: "Come, I will rehearse what God hath (really) prohibited you from: Join not anything as equal with Him; be good to your parents; kill not your children on a plea of want;- We provide sustenance for you and for them;- come not nigh to shameful deeds. Whether open or secret; take not life, which God hath made sacred, except by way of justice and law: thus doth He command you, that ye may learn wisdom" (Qur'an 6:151) .

the whole people: and if any one saved a life, it would be as if he saved the life of the whole people. (5:32)

Apart from the Qur'an, the Hadiths also have explicit references to suicide:

> *Bukhari Volume 2, Book 23, Number 445:*
>
> Narrated Jundab the Prophet said, "A man was inflicted with wounds and he committed suicide, and so God said: My slave has caused death on himself hurriedly, so I forbid Paradise for him."
>
> *Bukhari Volume 8, Book 73, Number 73:*
>
> Narrated Thabit bin Ad-Dahhak: "And if somebody commits suicide with anything in this world, he will be tortured with that very thing on the Day of Resurrection."
>
> Narrated Abu Huraira: The Prophet said, "He who commits suicide by throttling shall keep on throttling himself in the Hell Fire (forever) and he who commits suicide by stabbing himself shall keep on stabbing himself in the Hell-Fire."

Of course, the current context of terrorism and the influence of fundamentalism within Islam place some of the injunctions against suicide in direct conflict with those who would seek martyrdom in the name of faithfulness.

Like Judaism, the followers of Islam derive their resistance to taking one's own life from their theology, belief in the One God who gives and takes away life. To end life prematurely is to rob God of that power and, in most instances, to be captive to a prideful and unforgiveable pretense.

The Compromise of Compassion

And in the light of the injunctions against suicide, it is not surprising that every major western tradition holds it in contempt. But it is also true that, in many personal settings, religious leaders find themselves moved more by compassion than contempt. On the ground, suicide looks much different than it does in textbooks.

What are we going to say to the grieving parent who mourns the loss of a child? Of course, suicide is the denial of our sacred teachings, but the deep sorrow and anguish of those who are left behind call from us a profound sense of sorrow. It seems beside the point and more than a bit moralistic to cite commandments against suicide in the face of such sadness. Most leaders give their sacred teachings a pass and opt for the compromise of compassion for those who remain, since apart from everything else, The Creator of Heaven and Earth loves and cares for the creature.

And this situation becomes more complicated as we explore the question of medical assistance in dying, since the boundaries of life and death continue to change. It is no longer a simple matter of the cessation of vital signs. The questions of how and when we die deserve greater scrutiny, and we turn to that now.

Chapter 3

ADVANCING OUR LIVING OR PROLONGING OUR DYING

> Everyone knows they're going to die, but nobody believes it. . . . Learn how to die, and you learn how to live.
> —Mitchell Albom[1]

The Need for Dialectical Thinking

"Sir, please!" The student's hand was waving as he spoke. I hardly had time to set my books on the lectern. Welcome to the first days of class!

There is nothing more sobering than standing in front of 120 undergraduates who expect you to be entertaining, wise, captivating, and compassionate, every week for two semesters—at 8:30 in the morning. Daunting for even the best lecturers.

"Sir!" Louder now. This fellow is worried I'll miss his question.

---

1. Albom, *Tuesdays with Morrie*, 80, 83.

ADVANCING OUR LIVING OR PROLONGING OUR DYING

As I point toward him, inviting him to speak, I think again how, in many ways, as professors, we're frauds, allowing students to believe we know more than we do, feigning a level of intelligence we can rarely attain. From my place at the front of the class, I know that real knowledge is often the result of a dialogue. When I am honest, I will admit that much of what passes for wisdom in my answers to life's tough dilemmas depends almost entirely on the intelligence of the one asking the question. So, it is with some hope, and not a small measure of apprehension, that I invite this young man, the brightest light in my introductory ethics course, to ask his question.

For the first few lectures, we had been exploring the principle of forgiveness, and I could see he was very engaged and eager. Standing at the back of the room, he rose confidently and spoke—and not just to me, but to the whole class when he asked his question. "My girlfriend cheated on me last night. Should I forgive her?"

Talk about throwing a bomb into a crowded room. Every ear was on him. I checked around the room and noted that the girlfriend in question had decided not to attend class. No doubt, she'd hear about the debate later. Was this his revenge? Was he seriously wanting an answer, some way to move forward and resolve what was, arguably, a very painful predicament? Or was he merely using this classroom as a platform to vent his anger, perhaps even revel in the role of the wounded victim and, given the ubiquity of university gossip, to punish his ex?

There was no way to pick my way through the minefield of his motivations, so I took the question at face value. Since the university in question was founded by the Roman Catholic Church, there was no problem with first quoting Jesus, who, I reminded the student, had been asked roughly the same question. His answer had been to forgive not just seven times, but seventy times seven (Matt 18:22). Behind his formula was the bald truth that forgiveness is not an exact science. It does not keep count. Likewise, injury is not magically resolved by the passage of certain milestones. The desire for vengeance is real. It does not have a best before date.

However, it is usually useless. Rather than bringing resolution and peace, getting revenge simply perpetuates the cycle of violence and injustice. "The pathway forward is to find the courage to forgive."

Clearly, my student wanted more. "But she hurt me and betrayed us. She said we were meant for each other, and we started to talk of something more than a casual, one-night fling, and then she does this. It's unforgiveable." He wasn't crying, not outwardly at any rate, but he was clearly not pretending either. His heart was broken. There were a few titters from the other men in the back row, and a couple of young women in the front row started texting feverishly. The student sat back down in his chair, feeling a bit foolish and very vulnerable.

If we had been in my office in a private consultation, I would have delved more into his damaged heart and asked about the promises they had shared. How deep is the anguish? What does her betrayal really mean? But in a public forum, one is confined to more theoretical responses, and I sensed it was a good time to explore a primary ethical principle: dialectics.

Calming down those who would make fun of the student and giving a meaningful stare to the ones who were texting, I regained everyone's attention. "There are two things I can say about forgiveness: First, there are no second chances. Second, there are always second chances."

The student rose to his feet again, about to protest, when I continued, "Your girlfriend has robbed your trust, and there's no way around that. It hurts. There are no second chances. You can't turn back the clock of trust and get it back, can you? What's done is done, and no amount of wishing it otherwise will ever change the fact that she broke faith. You and she will have to live with the consequences, and it may well be that your relationship is now beyond redemption. Life is like that. Some actions shut the door. This is true particularly of physical injuries. Some wounds are beyond healing. The end. And I am sorry that at your relatively young age you have had to learn such a tough lesson. There are no second chances."

"But," the young man stuttered. . .

"And yet, there are always second chances," I continued. "Life is not a scripted plot beyond alteration. From the tradition of Christianity, I would point out that we do not believe in fate—a prescribed, unalterable pattern of events. 'Grace,' if it means anything, says that we can always find a way to start over. Your love will not be the same, of course, but this does not mean it can't be both meaningful and long-lasting. The cycle of life and love is a dance between light and dark, night and day. And with every new sunrise there is the potential of a grace-filled, new beginning."

To his credit, the student patiently waited until I had finished. Then he took a deep breath and allowed his emotions to speak again. "But I want a 'yes' or 'no.' Is that too much to ask? Do I forgive her or not?"

In those impulsive words, he was expressing the basic desire of the human heart: let's find a clear resolution. Surely there is a "right" or "wrong" decision. In matters of love, it is a keen desire. Isn't that the nature of truth: the clear delineation of one position over all others?

With the rise of "Trumpism" and a more rigid view of race relations and human dynamics, immigration and healthcare (to name just a few of our current stumbling blocks), this one-dimensional approach to "truth" is enjoying a resurgence. I recall a bumper sticker that proclaimed: "The Bible said it. I believe it. That settles it."

What I wanted this young student to recognize is that much of what we call "truth" within the human heart is discovered only by way of what philosophers call "dialectical" thinking. A big word and a big meaning. To achieve wisdom, we learn to hold together a "yes" and "no" at the same time. "Yes, you can try to forgive." "No, you cannot make forgiveness happen just because you want it." It's a both/and wisdom.[2]

Over the past few months, while I have been researching and writing about medical assistance in dying, I realize it is an area where this kind of dialectical thinking is essential. In the interviews

---

2. If you want to hear more on forgiveness, I would refer you to an article I wrote on forgiveness for the *United Church Observer*. See Levan, "Conundrum."

with many people who have been facing the crushing decision of ending the life of a loved one, whether by legal means under the new regime of Medical Assistance in Dying or in some less than lawful fashion, I have discovered that there are no easy answers. "Yes, we want our mother to live forever." "No, she can't suffer through much more." "Yes, a dignified death would be a blessing." "No, we don't want to hasten their end." "Yes, they are suffering too much." "No, they don't want to leave us." "Yes, they want the pain to end." "No, they accept what God gives them." "Yes, I want them to get relief." "No, I don't want them to die."

Learning how to die, like learning how to love, is a complex, dialectical dance. It's not a simple question, and there are no easy answers. I know you will want to explore both sides, as we face our ending faithfully.

As mentioned in the last chapter, the dominant position taken by the Abrahamic theological traditions is that ending a life intentionally is contrary to the will of Creation and the Creator. "Thou shalt not kill." However, it was noted that, in certain instances, taking life is nevertheless justifiable: in the defense of self for instance or when carrying out God's explicit command, as in the case of a Holy War scenario. The more complex theory of "justifiable war" was also explored in the last chapter with the conclusion being that ending life is both forbidden and condoned. It's a dialectic.

There was also an interesting interpretation of the sixth commandment that argued that the Hebrew word "kill" in the injunction was better translated as "murder." In that case, the taking of life arises from an explicit desire to do harm, to eliminate another human being. There is no concurrence or kindness. Murdering someone is an act of violence perpetrated to rob an individual of the gift of life against their will and is often used as punishment for perceived wrongdoing or as proof of one's superior status and power. Murder shuts down consent and ignores compassion. Medical assistance in dying is the exact opposite. Yes, ending life preemptively is contrary to God's intentions, but no, God does not expect or wish for human beings to suffer. So, there is an

ADVANCING OUR LIVING OR PROLONGING OUR DYING

injunction against dying and at the same time a preferential option for compassion.

Nevertheless, despite the dialectical tension of ending life, we come to the question of medical assistance in dying with a considerable resistance. It is born of the primary affirmation of the Abrahamic tradition that God is the Lord of living and dying. There is the underlying affirmation that life is a gift. It is not ours to decide, and so we proclaim along with Job that "God gives and takes life." This governance of living and dying is the sole prerogative of the Creator. It's God's move. And we tell ourselves that no matter how much we believe we are capable of those decisions, humanity is still morally ill-equipped and not yet spiritually capable of playing in this divine game.

That said, humanity has never acquiesced before disaster, saying that it is God's will and must be accepted. As I write this, the devastation wreaked by Hurricane Irma (fall 2017) is just coming to light. The loss of property is staggering, and given the widespread devastation, it is truly incredible that more people were not killed by the passing of this historic storm.

One of the striking pictures was taken before the winds hit. It was the shot of a packed, congested Floridian highway . . . cars bunched up, driving on the shoulder, using the opposite lanes—people fleeing the coming death-dealing disaster. Now one could argue that those who were so desperate to avoid injury and death were running from the will of God—like Jonah the prophet who fled from God's call. Surely the storm was God's will. Its intensity might be attributed to global warming, but the fact of hurricanes is clearly part of the divine creative prerogative.

God does hurricanes! Not humans!

That being the case, why don't we stay in place and take what Irma must dish out. Isn't that God's will? As I write that sentence, I realize that it sounds ridiculous, if not cruel and inhuman. We were birthed in love for the purpose of loving, and our life on earth is not a foregone conclusion, as if we have no part in its ongoing development. Life is a dialogue, or as I said above, a "dialectic," between the Creator's will and purpose and our own individual ability and determination. God grants life and human beings live it.

Surely, we believe that God oversees living and dying, all birth and death, and yet at the same time we have to agree that God is not in charge alone. Human beings, to the best of their ability, cooperate with the creative force, with the evolution of the species, with the momentum of the universe or put simply . . . with God. It's a yes/no dance.

Yes, God is in charge. No, we are not owners of our lives. Yes, human beings are responsible for the management of this earth. No, we do not undertake this stewardship alone. Ultimately, the earth is not ours to do with as we will, death included.

So, when we speak about medical assistance in dying, the Abrahamic tradition would invite us into a dialogue, a relationship. The God encountered in sacred scripture is not demanding adherence to doctrine or creedal confessions. The God of scripture is a God of love, mercy, and justice, and through time human beings have been in conversation with our God about what that means for human living and dying.

As the hurricane illustrates, it is not simply a matter of deciding God's will and putting up with it. God controls death, and yet God wills life. So how do human beings orchestrate the preservation of life in the fluid and often confusing claims and counter claims of existence?

Here's a simple example. I have just said God wills life for all. If someone is dying by inches, slowing losing muscle control and the ability to communicate, as is the case with ALS, is that really the life God wills? It looks a great deal more like punishment, when someone is completely aware of their surrounding yet unable to move even the smallest muscle, communicating only with blinks. Must that person wait through the increasing pain to the moment when the muscles controlling breathing will fail and he or she suffocates to death, gasping for their last breath alone? Is this virtue? Is that life? It sounds more like death. And since we cooperate with God in our living, is there something intrinsically wrong with also cooperating with God in our dying? Must we just stand alone and take it. We would not suggest that to those fleeing a hurricane! Why can that not be the same principle for those facing the stormy torments of ALS?

Advancing Our Living or Prolonging Our Dying

And yet while we might want to leave the whole debate about living and dying in God's hands, when we bring our ethical thinking to the bedside, our reasoning is further confounded by a disarmingly simple question. How do we distinguish between life and death? What criteria do we use to define living, and when are we in the process of dying? How do we distinguish the point at which we cease human intervention and allow God's purposes to proceed?

Before answering, let us explore a common ending. This happened several years ago. I was called to the intensive care unit of our local hospital. A parishioner's husband had a massive stroke. He'd had heart problems before, and so this was not entirely unexpected. He was in intensive care, and I met the family in the waiting room beside that unit. They'd been given the news that things "did not look very good." We gathered up our courage and went in "for a prayer," and we saw a man breathing through a tube, assisted by a ventilator. His chest rose and fell, his heart was beating, but he was unconscious. Apart from my affirmation that he was present with us in spirit, there was no evidence that he was aware of anything.

So, when we returned to the waiting room the question came quickly, "Does he want to live like this?" Younger members of the family held out hope that he would come out of it. He always broke through obstacles. "Give him a chance." His wife was more sanguine, "He's really gone this time." Some thought we could "pull the plug," because he would never want to be a "burden," while others were wanting to "give him a chance." And while this may seem like theoretical debating, it was made all the more real when the ICU nurse came in to ask about "heroic measures?" Had he made a living will? Were there advanced directives? Did anyone know if he wanted to be resuscitated if he experienced a further cardiac incident?

The issue seems so simple and yet so disarmingly difficult: Is the person in the next room alive or not? Is he living or dying? His chest was rising and falling with the sophisticated help of advanced medical technology, but was that life? A dozen years ago, he would have been dead. Now we faced a dilemma. Was the existence of some small brain activity really evidence of his living or the last vestiges of his dying?

Just as we are trying to understand the beginning of life within the confines of the debate over abortion, we cannot avoid a similar problem at the other end of life. What really represents death? Is it the cessation of brain waves or the unconscious muscle movements like breathing? Is it when the heart ceases to function on its own? Is dying complete when the individual is no longer able to communicate, falling into a deep coma from which there is no response? Or does death come earlier, when the person's spirit ceases to move abroad and there is no recognition of the love and care that surrounds us?

What is death?

In 1968, an *ad hoc* committee from Harvard University established four criteria for defining death:[3]

1. Unreceptivity and lack of responsiveness. There is total unawareness to externally applied stimuli and inner need, and complete unresponsiveness—irreversible coma. Even the most painful stimuli evoke no vocal or other response, not even a groan, withdrawal of a limb, or quickening of respiration.

2. No movement or breathing. Observation by physicians, covering a period of at least one hour, is adequate to satisfy the criteria of no spontaneous muscular movements, no spontaneous respiration, and no response to stimuli such as pain, touch, sound, or light.

---

3. Barnard, *Good Life*, 31–32.

3. No reflexes. Irreversible coma with abolition of central nervous system activity is evidenced in part by the absence of elicitable reflexes. The pupil will be fixed and dilated and will not respond to a direct source of bright light.
4. Flat encephalogram. Of great confirmatory value is a flat isoelectric EEG. We must assume that the electrodes have been properly applied, that the apparatus is functioning normally, and that the staff in charge is competent.

Using this criteria, it is quite possible to identify the moment when life ceases, though modern technology can sustain a biological functioning in spite of some of these circumstances. But the question arises, should we allow individuals to descend to this point before we declare their end has come? Is death simply the final step in a longer process of dying, and is there really virtue in allowing every stage of this dying to unfold without intervening? Does this final step differ from person to person? Some may embrace more pain and suffering than others. And what place does an individual's choice play in this process?

And this, certainly, is the key ethical issue we face currently. Clearly, we have already decided as a society not to stand by and watch the process of dying without interfering in the progression of what is inevitable. Narcotics, various surgical interventions, and physical therapies are used to "ease the pain" and to make the patient "comfortable." Ethically, we have decided that it is not virtuous to let dying take its course without attempting to offer compassionate relief.

As we grow greater awareness of the process of dying, we will be able to distinguish the moment when we slip from extending our living into prolonging our dying. And once that point has been reached, then surely we can employ a different set of tools to ease and comfort those who are close to their end.

What is at issue in the process of dying is a distinction that has not been examined sufficiently: the difference between biology and spirit. How often have I been at a bedside and the medical practitioner shakes their head, not able to understand how someone can continue living given the empirical evidence. They often shake their head and mumble something about spiritual strength but have no other wisdom to offer. They can't be blamed. Modern, western medical practice focuses almost exclusively on physiological health and rarely touches on emotional and spiritual well-being. And it is to a greater examination of this distinction that we now turn.

Chapter 4

CURING THE DISEASE VS. HEALING THE ILLNESS

> There is nothing undignified in choosing to allow an illness to run its full course.
> What is undignified is denying people suffering intolerably their right to choose otherwise.[1]
>
> —Michael Short,
> Journalist and *The Age* opinion editor

Healed and Dead

Where does time go? It was forty-two years ago this summer that I first encountered mortality. What began as a persistent but mild ache in my gut—as if I had tightened my belt one notch too many—progressed into an annoying side-splitting distress. After a hot bath designed to soothe all my body's toils and

---

1. See Short, "Why Australia Should Allow."

troubles, this trouble did not go away. I found myself on the way to the local ER where a helpful doctor told me, having touched a few tender spots and taken a couple of telling x-rays, that I had to have my appendix out. "It's close to bursting," she said. "And if we don't get it out now, it could prove fatal."

"Fatal?" Since when did I become "fatal?" Up until that point, I had been a young, immortal guy who never doubted that his body would perform as designed forever. What did I do wrong? Is this the start of the inevitable decline I saw in others but never imagined would happen to me?

On the way to the operating room, the medical orderly assured me this was routine and I would be "right as rain," and apart from wondering why rain was "right," I pondered for the first time my own ending. Will there come a time when I am not?

A bit melodramatic on my part. It was hardly a life-threatening procedure. Friday night on a long weekend. Since no one else needed immediate care, I was in and out before I had a chance to call my parents and warn them I was in the hospital.

In those days, an appendectomy required a few days of hospital care, and since the holiday weekend precluded any possibility of being discharged, they told me I would be a patient at least until Tuesday. They took me to a four-person, post-operative ward, where others who had undergone surgery recently were recuperating.

I was wheeled in beside an older man who told me that he had been fighting cancer. "It's gone into my guts and that will be the end of me," he said, frankly. No joking. The medical staff also were quite clear with him. There was no mincing of words. "We're afraid there is no possibility of reversing the spread of your cancer." They didn't say, "You're dying," but that was what they meant. The once hoped-for cure was not going to happen. Cancer wins.

This man's condition, regrettable as it could be, was compounded by the fact that when they changed his dressings, our room was filled with such a stench that everyone and everything that could leave, did so. The visitors went out the door, the hospital attendants who could wait to do their thing until his bandages were firmly back in place, found pressing business at the nursing station. I am sure if the wallpaper could have peeled itself from the walls, it, too, would have left. Terrible. I could not move, so I was there with him, and I could see that the awful odor was killing him.

It was in his eyes. His spirit wilted every time the half-choking attendants, having taken off his dressing, unleashed his stink into the room. He knew he was repulsive. His body was betraying him to such an extent that he was absolutely and literally obnoxious. As bad as the smell was, this man's self-disgust was certainly murderous. He was a modern leper—an outsider even to himself. And the knowledge of his untouchability was an added burden to an already damning condition.

Here we can make a clear distinction. There is a disease killing this man: it is a physiological disorder—cancer. No holds barred; it was relentless. And there is a debilitating illness that arises from the disease. The illness is the sense of humiliation and isolation that the disease creates and unleashes.

There was little doubt about the disease. Cancer was robbing him of everything—his family, his friends, their love and affection—and there was no cure for this disease. He might be "fighting" it, as we like to say about those who live with cancer, but let's not be naïve. He would lose this battle and very soon. The illness, on the other hand, was his own personal repugnance and the humiliation he felt when he saw the revulsion of his family as they came to visit him. The younger grandchildren made no effort to mask their disgust, as they held their noses and complained. His children were more discrete, but clearly uncomfortable. Even his wife was having trouble, laying a discreet forefinger under her nose when she thought he wasn't looking. If the disease was bad, the illness was worse.

How painful to watch the death of this man, for he lay in unresolved shame. His body had let him down. He was no longer touchable and, by extension, not capable of receiving or giving love. In addition, his self-perception was in the toilet. In those last days of his living, he felt closer to being a dirty sewer pipe than the handsome, virile man of his earlier years.

Where were his former dignity and personal agency? Gone! The illness had taken away the "him" he knew. The "he" he was no longer existed.

All the shame and humiliation, the isolation and invisibility, were the result of his illness, and it was as concrete as the disease. His sense of embarrassment and isolation were spiritual, emotional states, of course, but real nonetheless. And it was obvious to me that he suffered as much from this illness as from the disease . . . both were killing him.

Now, I had been told that hospital staff were "run off their feet," so I didn't expect much to happen on that weekend. But early on that Saturday evening, I marveled that a young nurse, with a bath basin and towel, came into our room. I was sure she wasn't coming for me. And, sure enough, she stopped at my neighbor's bedside, pulled the privacy curtain and for an hour gave him a bed bath. I could still see his face around the edge of the curtain and he was transfigured . . . a broad smile spreading across his countenance.

Now, can we please push the pause button and look closely at this picture.

A man, who felt himself to be untouchable, an outcast non-being, was being caressed and cleaned by a young human being who made no attempt to flee or free herself from his side. Can you imagine how that felt?

My neighbor was healed! There is no question that this simple act of treating him like a man who requires bathing restored him back to his old self. He was not contagious as he had thought. He was restored!

Three hours later, he died, a healed man. The disease finally took him, but his illness was banished by the compassion and good will of that nurse. Looking back now, I see that she did what the sophisticated and well-equipped medical system could not: she healed his illness. The problem is that the very system we call "health care" is oriented and almost entirely given over to attacking and curing disease. And when those efforts fail, it tries to allay the symptoms of the disease with narcotics and painkillers. Very little time, resources or wisdom, is given to fighting the illness, let alone curing it. It's not that the health professionals are cold and heartless. They have not been explicitly trained to understand and address this distinction between disease and illness.

The thesis of this book is that a careful understanding of this difference will help when applied to medical assistance in dying. Before exploring that in greater depth, I would like to make a brief biblical digression to illustrate that this interplay between disease and illness is not just the product of an over fertile imagination.

Healing the Illness: Biblical Wisdom

Two gospel stories will be sufficient to explore the interplay between curing the disease and healing the illness, the first from Mark and the second from Luke. In each, there may be many possible meanings or insights we could draw from these passages, and while we might want to argue that each passage has a more important message than the one we examine, nonetheless it will become evident that this dynamic of healing the illness is an essential part of the fascination and wonder that Jesus inspired.

Before we can delve into each story, a few basic facts must be held in the back of our minds. The historical story of Jesus takes place in occupied territory. The Roman empire was the unavoidable backdrop to his words and deeds. It is not necessary to turn the Romans into heinous villains. They were occupiers, and they were hated by the general populace by virtue of the imposition of their cultural and political values, which in consequence curtailed the Jewish dreams and hopes. In occupied territory, everything has a political meaning—reflecting either in favor of the Romans or against them. No one and no thing was exempt from questions of resistance or collaboration.

The Jewish community enjoyed special status in the empire, not being required to pay tribute to civic deities and attend the otherwise prescribed public rituals and ceremonies. We can imagine that they were envied by some gentiles and hated by others. In either case, these Jews would appear to be stingy—having only one God. It is a small thing viewed from outside, but this unique place of Judaism was prized by those who enjoyed it. And it was with vigilance that the righteous preserved their identity as Jews. Keeping the Torah became not just a convenient anchor for one's daily routine, it was also a key to keeping one's very concrete and cherished security.

From the perspective of Temple Judaism of the first century, righteousness was preserved by regularly attending the prescribed rites and sacrifices in Jerusalem, adhering to the purity code in eating and cleaning, and preserving rigid boundaries against the unclean. All gentiles, heretics, Romans, and sex workers, were indelibly unclean. It mattered not a whit what they thought or believed or confessed. They were untouchable. Women having their period, people who buried or dealt with the dead, individuals who touched foreigners or their affairs, were all temporarily unclean and therefore suspect. For certain they would not be invited to dinner, apart from undertaking several prescribed cleansing rituals.

It is close to impossible to ascertain how the need for spiritual righteousness mingled with resentment toward Rome. In Jerusalem, where the stakes were high, any perception of bending to foreign values or idols was inflammatory. Out on the narrow alleys of a backwater, seaside town like Capernaum in southern Galilee, who knows how the balance was struck between staying righteous and getting by? We know Galilee was the modern equivalent of a Bible Belt and that it was fiercely protective of its status as a righteous, Jewish community. When we realize that the uprisings against Caesar that took place just before Jesus was born and in the years 66–72 had fervent support from Galileans, we might surmise that it was also a tough-minded, touchy tinderbox. In our current context, we would name it a "redneck" frontier.

CURING THE DISEASE VS. HEALING THE ILLNESS

We turn to the fifth chapter of Mark's gospel,[2] and there we read what some scholars call a "sandwich,"[3] in which one story is surrounded by two scenes of a second story. This is one of Mark's trademarks. He uses this technique often, and one can only guess what relationship he imagined existed between the two tales. In the "sandwich" found in chapter five, we could argue that both deal with a "sick" female. One is a young twelve year old—on the brink of womanhood—and we are told she is dying. The second is older

---

2. *Mark 5:21–43:* 21 When Jesus had crossed again in the boat to the other side, a great crowd gathered around him; and he was by the sea. 22 Then one of the leaders of the synagogue named Jairus came and, when he saw him, fell at his feet 23 and begged him repeatedly, "My little daughter is at the point of death. Come and lay your hands on her, so that she may be made well, and live." 24 So he went with him. And a large crowd followed him and pressed in on him. 25 Now there was a woman who had been suffering from hemorrhages for twelve years. 26 She had endured much under many physicians, and had spent all that she had; and she was no better, but rather grew worse. 27 She had heard about Jesus, and came up behind him in the crowd and touched his cloak, 28 for she said, "If I but touch his clothes, I will be made well." 29 Immediately her hemorrhage stopped; and she felt in her body that she was healed of her disease. 30 Immediately aware that power had gone forth from him, Jesus turned about in the crowd and said, "Who touched my clothes?" 31 And his disciples said to him, "You see the crowd pressing in on you; how can you say, 'Who touched me?'" 32 He looked all around to see who had done it. 33 But the woman, knowing what had happened to her, came in fear and trembling, fell down before him, and told him the whole truth. 34 He said to her, "Daughter, your faith has made you well; go in peace, and be healed of your disease." 35 While he was still speaking, some people came from the leader's house to say, "Your daughter is dead. Why trouble the teacher any further?" 36 But overhearing what they said, Jesus said to the leader of the synagogue, "Do not fear, only believe." 37 He allowed no one to follow him except Peter, James, and John, the brother of James. 38 When they came to the house of the leader of the synagogue, he saw a commotion, people weeping and wailing loudly. 39 When he had entered, he said to them, "Why do you make a commotion and weep? The child is not dead but sleeping." 40 And they laughed at him. Then he put them all outside, and took the child's father and mother and those who were with him, and went in where the child was. 41 He took her by the hand and said to her, "Talitha cum," which means, "Little girl, get up!" 42 And immediately the girl got up and began to walk about (she was twelve years of age). At this they were overcome with amazement. 43 He strictly ordered them that no one should know this, and told them to give her something to eat.

3. See Miller, ed., *Complete Gospels*, 24.

and has suffered for twelve years from constant hemorrhaging. Given that the menstrual blood was the sign of fertility, Mark may have joined these stories because they dealt with one girl, who was not yet a woman, and another, who was too much a woman.

The young girl is the daughter of Jairus, a synagogue official. One must imagine this man being a respected, wealthy patron of the local gathering hall or synagogue community—a righteous man beyond question. It was a sign of Jesus' popularity and the respect with which his healing was held that Jairus should approach him. This carpenter from Nazareth is a rising star!

Jesus agrees to go with this honored man to his home, and on the way, a woman, who according to the gospel "had been suffering from hemorrhages for twelve years," approached Jesus without his knowledge. Then we are told that "she had endured much under many physicians, and had spent all that she had; and she was no better, but rather grew worse." The constant issue of blood was not simply a painful condition, it also meant that she was an outsider—not allowed into any righteous household. According to the best common sense of that community, the constant flow of blood was a repugnant sign of her sinfulness. She was to be at the very least avoided. At worst, she should be ostracized. No wonder she had spent all she had to cure herself of this condition. She was untouchable. The disease was some form of hemophilia or gynecological disorder. And the illness was her isolation and shame. Each equally painful.

If we compare the two chief supplicants of these stories, we see a remarkable contrast. One is a wealthy man and the center of the community, respected and honored as a patron, someone everyone wanted to meet and perhaps befriend. The other was an impoverished woman, an outsider, repulsive and shunned by all who wished to preserve their religious identity and, by extension, their political security.

We are told this woman approaches Jesus, and without his permission or knowledge, she reaches out to touch just a bit of Jesus' garment—thinking that so strong is healing power that just a mere brush with his person will be enough. And sure enough, her blood flow ceases and she is cured of her disease. Hallelujah!

I can't explain how this cure happened, and there is little merit in trying to uncover its source. But what happens next I do understand. Jesus feels that healing power has left him and turns around asking who had touched him. The disciples scoff. In this crowd how do you avoid not being touched? Fighting her own fear, the woman comes forward and confesses, perhaps expecting to be scolded, punished or, horror of horrors, to have her disease reinstated. She is used to being rejected and rebuked.

Surprisingly, Jesus praises her for her faith. (She is perhaps shown to have more faith than the synagogue official who later may have some doubts about Jesus' healing power.)

If we look closely at what Jesus has done, we recognize that he breaks through the wall of the illness of segregation that this woman has suffered. In his presence, she is not a reject or contagion, but a shining example of trust—a model believer that the righteous man will be asked to imitate.

In these few words of affirmation, Jesus heals her illness. A spiritual leader has invited her back into the community, reestablished her place and secured her future. Whatever the source of the cure of her disease, we can see clearly that it was his compassion and forgiveness that were the agents of her healing. By breaking down barriers of gender-based, socio-theological prejudice, Jesus restored her health.

Turning to the gospel of Luke, we move forward several decades. The third evangelist is speaking to a community that has become established in their convictions about Jesus, and they enjoy some measure of security in their belief. Luke's purpose in writing his gospel is to tell his audience "an orderly narrative of the events that have their course among us."[4] That's what he said openly, but clearly his other agenda is to wake them up from their apathy. His stories often contain the kind of surprise that catches out the listener, contrasting what we have come to accept as truth against what Jesus tells us is the wisdom of God's household.

4. See Luke 1:1.

In the middle of his story, Luke has Jesus turn his path toward Jerusalem. This is the start of the passion. To leave Galilee and arrive in Jerusalem in the south, there are two routes righteous Jews would choose: one is to go west to the coast and travel down to Caesaria Maritima and then strike directly east to the holy city; the second option is to walk west into the wilderness and follow down the east side of the Jordan River, crossing at Jericho and mounting the infamous road up to Jerusalem. Both routes are designed to avoid one place: Samaria. That is where the hated and contagious heretics live. Samaritans are like the unfaithful brother who betrays the family trust and truth, more despised than those who have never known or cared about our treasured beliefs. And since one could be made unclean simply by walking in the shadow of a Samaritan, and given that they held the Jews in equal contempt, it was safer to avoid them all together. But in Luke's gospel, Jesus is walking down the knife edge between Judea and Samaria. Dangerous, if not foolhardy.

It is in this precarious place that ten lepers,[5] seeing Jesus, call to him from a distance. They do not come right up to the company of disciples, because in that world lepers were unclean and contagious. (Think of those infected with the Ebola virus.) Proper precautions are respected by all concerned. They plead for "mercy." Ask yourself, why would lepers ask for mercy? Why not ask to be cured? The simple answer is that leprosy (according to the Levitical code—Lev 13–14) is essentially a spiritual problem. It is evidence of God's disfavor, which is why it makes one unclean. It was also presumed to be punishment for some previous sin. Whether one

---

5. *Luke 17: 11-19:* 11 On the way to Jerusalem Jesus was going through the region between Samaria and Galilee. 12 As he entered a village, ten lepers approached him. Keeping their distance, 13 they called out, saying, "Jesus, Master, have mercy on us!" 14 When he saw them, he said to them, "Go and show yourselves to the priests." And as they went, they were made clean. 15 Then one of them, when he saw that he was healed, turned back, praising God with a loud voice. 16 He prostrated himself at Jesus' feet and thanked him. And he was a Samaritan. 17 Then Jesus asked, "Were not ten made clean? But the other nine, where are they? 18 Was none of them found to return and give praise to God except this foreigner?" 19 Then he said to him, "Get up and go on your way; your faith has made you well."

CURING THE DISEASE VS. HEALING THE ILLNESS

suffered from the actual disease of leprosy (and an examination of pertinent symptoms described in Leviticus might suggest the actual disease was anything from psoriasis to infected skin lesions), the source of one's cure was to be declared free of sin by a priest or temple official. Indeed, that is precisely what Jesus tells them. Presumably, having permission from such a well-known and respected spiritual leader like Jesus would be sufficient for lepers to get a hearing with the pertinent priests who might determine their cleanliness.

In this case, in Luke's gospel, the disease in question is some form of skin disorder. It could well be leprosy, but just as likely it was any variety of dermatological conditions. And the concomitant illness, as was the case with the woman in Mark's story, is isolation and shame. In both cases, people saw the betrayal of their body (too much blood or blemished skin) as evidence of their unworthiness and rejection by God and the community.

So, Jesus sends them off to the spiritual authority, and the ten lepers, getting this go-ahead, run off to receive their "cure." Only one returns to give thanks for his health, and here's the surprise. This lonely, grateful man is a Samaritan: the enemy! The person everyone knows is evil and beyond hope is the only one who offers proper thanks for the gift of his life.

In this story, we see Jesus addressing the illness first. Unlike others of his company who would have ignored the pleading of street people (who talks to panhandlers anymore?), Jesus stops and listens to their pleadings. He breaks through social and religious barriers. They are no longer outsiders and rejects. And receiving this healing of the illness, they are then able to go and seek a cure for their disease. In this case, quite particularly, the healing of the illness is the prerequisite of curing the disease . . . both essential.

The story has the added political message that the ones we call "enemies" are just as worthy to be brought into the community. Indeed, in their healing by being brought into God's household, we also receive our own healing from the prejudices that have separated us.

In each of these examples, I believe we can see the interplay between disease and illness and how the curing of the former brings about the healing of the latter and vice versa. Full recovery requires that we address both.

If the biblical evidence is not sufficient, I am reminded of my grandson's distress when he was helping peel the potatoes for our camping trip. He cut his fingers and came running asking for a Band-Aid. Now, we could simply apply this cure to his cut and let it go. But any parent knows that what is as important is the cuddle, the cooing words of comfort and a kiss or two to "make it better." We do this instinctively, but on closer examination, are we not just curing the disease (the cut) but also healing the illness (the child's fear and dismay)?

Is it possible to apply the same thinking and acting to the event of dying?

The Illness of Dying

The diseases of dying are well-known to a modern audience: cancer being chief among them. Then comes heart disease, Alzheimer's, ALS, kidney failure. And besides these physiological disorders, we fear the external "diseases" that bring about death: terrorist attacks, gun violence, road accidents, drug abuse. The list is long, and each holds its own terror. But is there also a list of dying illnesses?

What is the chief illness associated with dying? Is it not the sense of loss? Those who watch a loved one decline toward death are fraught with the sense of losing this specific one. No more will we be able to join them in conversations, in sharing common memories. With them goes a piece of our soul—a deep wound. But the person who is dying loses everything: spouse, friends, children, grandchildren—all their love and care, their esteem and gratitude . . . we lose everything. We cease to be, and everything that made us, who we are, is cast aside. The ultimate and final defeat of everything we are.

That is a terrible burden to bear. Even harder to endure.

CURING THE DISEASE VS. HEALING THE ILLNESS

After this striking aspect of the illness of dying, we might then list a few lesser issues. Most people fear the process of dying, the loss of dignity and control over their own functions and choices. There is a natural shedding of personal agency that dying requires, and it is quite fearful. We return to a time and position, much like our infancy, when we are more and more dependent on those who care for us to perform even the simplest of tasks: brushing teeth, mounting stairs, taking a bath. No one endures these aspects of the illness of dying willingly, and some of us fail to muster the grace to accept them honestly.

In both the illnesses of deep loss and growing indignity, there is a deeper fear: aloneness. Unlike any other human activity, including birth, dying is a solitary step. We walk the valley of the shadow on our own. And this is perhaps the hardest dimension of the illness of dying to endure. Our life has been enriched, even defined, by community, and this is now ultimate isolation.

And the obvious question: Can we heal the illness of dying? Is there a unique technique, a special approach, that brings healing even as we are doomed to die?

It is to that key question that we now turn.

Chapter 5

HEALING DEATH

> I ask my Master and Mistress to remember me always, but not to grieve for me too long. In my life I have tried to be a comfort to them in times of sorrow, and added joy in their happiness. It is painful for me to think even in death I should cause them pain. Let them remember that while no dog has had a happier life (and this I owe to their love and care of me), now that I have grown blind and deaf and lame and even my sense of smell fails me so that a rabbit could be right under my nose and I might not know, my pride has sunk to such a sick, bewildered humiliation. I feel life is taunting me with having over-lingered my welcome. It is time I say good-bye before I become too sick a burden on myself and on those who love me.[1]
>
> —Eugene O'Neill

---

1. O'Neill, *Last Will*, 3–4.

The Rhythm of Living

We were all holding golden lab puppies. Plenty to go around; the litter had begun with six healthy females and four males. Across from me is a teenager, being watched closely by her single mom. Beside me is another mother, her teenage son was still in the pool—didn't want to do any puppy time. With all of us occupied, cooing over the cute little dogs, the conversation turned to parenting. The single mother turned, and to make conversation she said, "If only our kids stayed this cute. It would be so much easier." I replied that every stage of rearing children is different and exciting, but neither parent believed me. Teenagehood was a pain, a serious strain on the cohesion of even the most stable families. My kids are now parents themselves, having babies. "The teen years are a flash in the pan." They shook their heads, while I continued, "They'll be gone before you know it and then they'll be married. There is something quite exciting watching your own kids take on the role of parent." They looked doubtful, so I added, "Seriously, they come back to you with fresh, enlightened appreciation."

Neither mother could even imagine a time without a grumpy, moody, crazy teenager to wrestle every day into civility. It's not their fault. When we're young, we don't recognize that life has a rhythm that cannot be denied. Our kids pass us by, and we hope they take what they have been given of our love and laughter and pass it along to their children.

One of the pains as we age is the realization that there comes a time when this rhythm starts to reverse itself, and the children become the caregivers (parents?) of their own mothers and fathers. And as we age, we devolve into more infantile realities: unable to walk, talk, or even control our bodily functions. It is at that stage that we grieve what we have lost and carry a heavy burden. In the quote above, Blemie, the family dog in Eugene O'Neill's household, puts it perfectly: "I feel life is taunting me with having over-lingered my welcome. It is time I say good-bye before I become too sick a burden on myself and on those who love me."[2]

2. O'Neill, *Last Will*, 3–4.

This points to two of the chief symptoms of the illness of dying: guilt and shame. None of us wants to encumber our children or their offspring. We were born to grow up and apart. Healthy people resist the transition back into a dependent state. Everyone wants to leave the party before the music stops, so to speak. What an embarrassment to overstay our welcome so that the hosts become restless, wondering how much longer we will stay.

Besides the emotional toll imposed on children of aging parents, there are some very practical considerations. Given the cost of health care and home visits from medical professionals, there is a very concrete problem of inordinately depleting inheritances by loitering too long on the brink of dying. I recall my mother's case. She served tea to the emergency room social worker on a Friday afternoon, and they mapped out the next few months of fees, charges, and prescriptions that my mom's treatment would entail. It was an astronomical sum. By Saturday, she was back in hospital and died on Monday morning. It seems clear that she had decided that she would not bankrupt her estate and had given in to dying gracefully.

And while no one wants to die—that's to be expected—it's the process of dying that is worrisome. There are some good reasons to leave this earthly life before our condition becomes unbearable for those around us. And a healing death is one that relieves the dying person of their shame and guilt, and any sense of desperation that they feel.

The final symptom of dying—isolation—is not easily dismissed. There is no getting around the solitary nature of this final event of our living. In fact, dying is the only human activity that we must do on our own. But it can be alleviated slightly by the presence of those with whom we have shared memories and affections. And this is just common sense. Most people recognize that there is something essential about being at the deathbed of those we love. What do we say, "No one should die alone!"

And while medical assistance in dying does not address the isolation that is a key aspect of the illness of dying, in other respects it may well be that it could be used as one instrument or procedure that addresses the other symptoms of the illness of dying and therefore help health professionals carry out some measure of healing.

Taking Our Dying Seriously

As I write this chapter, Knut, my wife's father, is declining toward his end: a tumor behind his right eye is counting down his time. Relentless. There is no turning back the clock, no possible remission or curing of this disease. Knut is now ninety-four, and he's been a healthy adult, cross country skiing up until a few years ago. So, his body is strong, but this cancer will kill him, and no one is talking about him "getting better."

The illness of dying, in Knut's case, is his sensory isolation: the complete loss of sight, confounded by his loss of hearing. His days are spent in silence, sitting in his nursing home room. The staff of this veterans facility are excellent, and the accommodation is clearly a step up from the institutional care we imagine happens in many underfunded nursing homes. But he suffers loneliness and isolation. His mind is sharp, but his outside world is shrinking.

I have watched as my wife and her siblings try to address their father's illness: how do we give him the best quality of life that is possible? Will regular caregivers or visiting friends help? How about trips to his beloved church? And while I am impressed with their thoroughness, it is clear that they are making it up as they go along. No one has any experience or expertise. And the staff are likewise not equipped with the training or experience to make suggestions on how to proceed. They're guessing as much as we are.

What Knut's case indicates is that we do not take our dying as seriously as we take our living. If we step back and examine public resources and academic orientation, all our energies (both intellectual and economic) are exclusively fixed on the preservation of life, the curing of disease and the accommodation of people who must live with irremediable conditions. Very little attention is paid to equipping families or health care professionals with the practical and serviceable means to alleviate the well-known, but under-studied, symptoms of the illness of dying. For example, to use my father-in-law again as an example, surely we can gather together a manual of best practices for relieving sight-impaired, aging seniors. It's not like it's a rare occurrence. How about aroma therapy tools for the hard of hearing? Smell was the primary sense that Knut enjoyed, until his tumor blocked much of his ability. So now we're asking about quality of living, when most senses are impaired. How do we achieve meaning? Touch therapy? The point is that no one has given it much thought. We're reduced to *ad hoc* measures that may or may not address his illness.

It is to inspire more concerted thought and action in working through both the physical and emotional/spiritual process of dying that I have written this text. Knut's spirit of determination is an inspiration. Surely, we can concentrate some of our considerable public resources to developing protocols and procedures, "for helping people end their life with fullness and peace."

Medical assistance in dying should therefore not be seen as a final solution to the quality of living at the end of life. Nor is it the only one. It is merely one tool among many to "heal death." All too often I have seen it embraced without careful exploration of what might constitute better pathways to healing.

Chapter 6

CAUTIONS

The Defense of the Vulnerable

> Commitment is not easily espoused in a society that celebrates self-determination and the individual's inalienable rights. The power of individualism in North America mitigates against the prospect that a person might suspend his or her autonomy long enough to permit the claims of faith-tradition to make their impact. In short, commitment goes against the grain of a social milieu that has apotheosized freedom, glorified the free-ranging individual whose only 'commitment' is to his or her own unrelenting pursuit of personal happiness.[1]
>
> —John Douglas Hall

The "OOOOh" Factor

At the ripe age of sixty-five, I decided to have my midlife crisis. Perhaps it's my second. I resigned from a comfortable job in

---

1. Hall, *Professing the Faith*, 25.

the heart of the largest city in Canada, left a loving and forgiving congregation, where I knew most of the stories and hence had a relatively easy time navigating the emotional ups and downs that are the constant work in ministry. I was driving away from a large urban community in which cultural and intellectual stimulation abounded. My grandchildren were nearby. High-speed Internet, subway transit, and dedicated bike lanes were at my beck and call. A perfect life. And I left it all to take up a new mission in a church on Salt Spring Island off the southern coast of British Columbia.

To Americans, this may seem like an adventure into the uncharted wilderness, but to Canadians, it is another story. I would mention to folks down east where I was headed, and to a person who said, "OOOOh . . . that will be great." Salt Spring Island is fixed in our northern imagination as a piece of paradise, separated from the noisy bustle of modernism, nestled up against the beauty of the Rocky Mountains, but floating in a blue sea teaming with orcas. This island is renowned for its concentration of artists and writers[2] and having none of the inclement weather that plagues the rest of the country. It is the wilderness with the bugs removed, so to speak. Close enough to the frontier to offer personal freedom and in easy reach of Vancouver and Victoria—both of which have very good opera—what more could you ask? It's "OOOOh," so nice.

In the past, the Gulf Islands in general, and Salt Spring Island in particular, were understood to be like a last frontier, basking in a pioneering promise of "doing your own thing." This island was the destination of free spirits who wanted to build "off the grid," experiment with passive solar power and composting toilets, all the while not having to worry about the ravages of winter. No snow—that's big. For Canadians, our climate is divided into two major periods: skiing season and bad skiing season. Snow is a constant.[3]

---

2. A 2017 study showed this fact. Salt Spring Island Foundation, "Salt Spring Island's Vital Signs," 17.

3. In 1965, a Quebecois musician, Gilles Vigneault, wrote a song that became an unofficial national anthem, "Mon pays, ce n'est pas un pays, c'est l'hiver." Translated as: "My country is not a country, it's winter."

So, to be without that pressure is paradise. It's as if we cheated the weather gods.

While much has changed on this island since it was invaded by freedom-loving hippies, there is still a spirit of individualism in the air. There are no fashion statements or faddish trends on Salt Spring Island, except that anything and everything is acceptable. Self-determination rules, and the biggest complaint is the restrictiveness of things like building codes and water conservation stipulations.

And while I rejoice in the "OOOOh" factor of this place and love the weather, I am struck by the need to honor our limits. Perhaps the changing climate and the threat of summers without rain and the need to collect and conserve water will bring us all to appreciate the wisdom of restraint. Our biggest challenge is to discern when and how to constrain personal autonomy. And this becomes doubly difficult in a society that accepts individual freedom as an unassailable virtue. As the French philosopher Jacques Ellul states in the quote introducing this chapter, we live in a world that has "glorified the free-ranging individual whose only 'commitment' is to his or her own unrelenting pursuit of personal happiness." So how do you articulate the need for limits, when our culture worships individual freedom?

It is precisely this domination of heroic individualism that raises one or two major cautionary notes regarding medical assistance in dying. And what begins as a largely philosophical debate arrives very quickly at some practical and poignant questions.

Where's the Line?

In theory, everyone is in favor of relieving pain.

"We shoot horses, don't we?" That's the response of Phyllis Elliott my faithful counsel at church. In answer to my question about medical assistance in dying, she replied with her typical common sense, "Surely we can show mercy to fellow beings who are suffering."

Choosing the time of your own death has always been possible, but until the recent implementation of Bill C-14, it was both illegal and immoral. As noted above in chapter 2, the Abrahamic tradition has an aversion to "playing God." We previously considered that ending one's life was a selfish, presumptive act. How dare we rewrite the providential play book! Our nation's Criminal Code and our common vocabulary reflected that position. You don't "do" suicide, you "commit" it, because, apart from everything else, it was a crime.

But, as Phyllis intuited, everyone will concede that compassion trumps law, when someone is declining into intolerable suffering. So, if you're living with ALS for instance, you get a pass. Likewise, in the later stages of cancer. No one should have to endure the indignity and pain that some terminal diseases entail.

Now we have a clear path. Under certain circumstances, it is possible to choose your own death. It's not for everyone. However, we would be naïve if we did not recognize that granting this possibility to individuals changes us as a society. We are not the same, even though we think that this is just a small, legislative acknowledgement of a commonly held position.

Apart from the resistance to playing God, giving an individual the permission to end their own life grants to that person a level of personal control that was hitherto both impractical and unattainable. A century ago, based on the presumption of an inalienable right to life, society, as a whole, held the authority to control living and dying. There was no quarter granted to any who wanted to short-circuit this foundational right of life given to those who are living. Society had the power to legislate individual "rights" within this ultimate "right," but it never granted an "override."

Nevertheless, with the advent of the debate around abortion, this fundamental "social" right to life for the living was tested and successfully challenged. In some circumstances, individuals could choose to end an unwanted or dangerous pregnancy. Legal abortions changed us as a society. It was now possible that an individual choice could trump social authority. And without probing the pros and cons of abortion, the fact is we are now changed as a community. It is quite possible to question social authority and to assume that a plea for upholding an individual "right" will be taken seriously. Indeed, the Charter of Rights and Freedoms has entrenched this possibility within law. We are no longer a society which protects all human beings against all unwarranted incursions into their personal security and safety. There are times when individual human rights supersede social authority. A hotly debated example of this shift can been witnessed in MRI waiting rooms, where individuals can jump the queue and avoid the long line-ups to the publically funded procedure by paying to go to a private clinic. My right to have my medical results, when I want them, takes priority over society's triage-based allocation of medical resources.

Of course, we do not want nor do we have an autocratic state in North America. No one wants to give society an unassailable authority to grant life to the living. Heteronomy (the rule of law from outside the individual) cannot be absolute. We cherish our autonomy (the rule of law from within the individual) too much. And so, we have developed compromises, balances of power, allowing more or less autonomy to individuals depending on the people's perceptions and political choices.

I spoke of the need for dialectical thinking in ethical decision making, and this is where it is most required. Heteronomy and autonomy must be kept in tension, neither triumphing over the other. And the questions become how to orchestrate this tension. With the passage of Bill C-14, we have swung considerable weight behind personal autonomy. And while most people in society would grant the necessity of relieving suffering, the need for limiting that relief is also accepted as reasonable. Liberal individualism cannot surpass all other considerations. Where is the line drawn around personal choice?

Here is an example that points out this predicament: In 1993, Robert Latimer, a Saskatchewan farmer, killed his severely disabled twelve-year-old daughter, Tracy, by piping exhaust fumes into the cab of his truck. His defense was that his daughter (whose communication skills were limited) was unable to continue to suffer through the medical procedures and treatment regimes that had been such a dominant part of her short life. It was better to relieve her of her suffering. Mr. Latimer claimed it was a mercy killing, and, like Phyllis, he understood we treat our animals with the compassion to end their life when they are beyond hope. Why could he not offer his daughter the same kindness and relief?

It is with that troubling parent's dilemma of when and how to relieve pain for a child we love that I conclude this chapter. It illustrates perfectly that this is not an easy nor straightforward decision. It requires, as I have said several times, the dialectical thinking that holds several truths together at the same time, without diminishing any.

Chapter 7

RECOMMENDATIONS
A Funeral Rehearsal

Certainly, suffering at the end of life is sometimes unavoidable and unbearable, and helping people end their misery may be necessary. . . . But we damage entire societies if we let providing this capability divert us from improving the lives of the ill. Assisted living is far harder than assisted death, but its possibilities are far greater, as well.[1]

—Atul Gawande

Old age should burn and rave at close of day.[2]

—Dylan Thomas

1. Gawande, *Being Mortal*, 31.
2. Thomas, "Do Not Go Gentle."

Introduction: Keeping Our Eyes on the Prize

Death has a finality that is difficult to match in any other sphere of human existence. Once we cross over, there is no turning back, no returns or exchanges, no second chance. For one who is dying, it is the end of everything that has been. Given that finality, one might well be advised that the best approach to medical assistance in dying is to improve our assistance in living. Death will take us easily enough. Living fully until that time requires considerably more imagination and courage than taking that final step into the darkness. And it is to improve our creative response to death that I offer a story of one family's imaginative use of the time that was left to them.

But before I conclude an examination of the question of medical assistance in dying, I feel constrained to declare my position. Along with Dylan Thomas, I would claim that one need not acquiesce before that "good night." The human voice raised against the night is one of the most noble I know. Hence, let what we do until that moment speak of our courage to rage against the overtaking darkness. The fact that we can now ask for medical assistance to end unbearable suffering should make us all the more poignantly committed to living in the light and not to accept the darkness too easily.

Minor Recommendations

Before the concluding story, there are a few minor recommendations that have come to light in the course of this research . . . matters to explore as we become more refined in the application of this form of healing.

In the light of our need to seek constant and consistent consent, the law provides that "immediately before providing the medical assistance in dying, give the person an opportunity to withdraw their request and ensure that the person gives express consent to receive medical assistance in dying."[3]

3. See Appendix 2, "Bill C-14," 101.

RECOMMENDATIONS

This condition was put in place to avoid the unfortunate circumstance in which an individual might have second thoughts or that, having asked for the treatment, their condition changes to the extent that they do not want to die immanently. In theory, that seems to be a reasonable condition, and in many circumstances, it may perform the function it was designed to meet. However, in many cases of advanced cancer treatment, the patient is essentially drugged to sleep to avoid suffering, and this condition requires that they be awakened from a pain-free state to give their consent a second time. It is questionable whether that "awakening" is necessary. Is it not cruel and unusual punishment to wake someone up into a state of deep anguish, and can we really be reassured that someone who is thus brought back to excruciating pain is really of sound mind? Does the legislation not contain a basic contradiction—offering relief from pain while requiring a patient to undergo it in order to avoid it?[4] Surely there are means to giving the patient a "second chance" to back out of the treatment that do not include inflicting pain just prior to the death that we say is prescribed to relieve the very pain we are making the patient suffer.

In a similar vein the legislation requires that a patient make a written request to have medical assistance in dying and that this "request was signed and dated by the person—or by another person under subsection(4)—before two independent witnesses who then also signed and dated the request."[5]

Again, that seems reasonable. Another check on hasty or uninformed consent. But if we think of the reality, many patients at this stage in their life would have difficulty finding "independent" witnesses. Trapped in a care home or confined to their hospital bed, to whom do they turn? The only people they know and see are either medical staff involved in their case or family members who can hardly be called "independent." One family told me of the distressing hardship of, having finally been given the permission

---

4. As mentioned above, it was precisely this legislative contradiction that caused Rob Oliphant, MP, the co-chair of the parliamentary committee, to vote against the law when it was put before the House of Commons.

5. See Appendix 2, "Bill C-14," 100.

for their mother to end her life, having to go into the lobby of her high-rise to search for strangers who would witness her written request. It's a minor inconvenience perhaps, but it speaks to the dignity of the one who is dying that total strangers have to be roped into another human being's last request in order for that request to be legitimate. There must be a way to have witnesses to a document that does not require this kind of disquieting use of strangers.

1. I recall, upon first hearing of this legislation, thinking that one of the horror stories of dying would be solved. How often have I visited nursing homes and long-term care homes and watched as the hallways fill with patients who are no longer with us, drooling away their last few years in absolute isolation? This law has nothing to say to the fear of being reduced to a vegetative state. An ICU nurse friend once said that she was going to pack her hospital suitcase with a sign to be posted above her bed in the event that the operation goes south and she were to be turned into a vegetable: "Step on the air tube," her sign read. There's an urban legend that someone had "do not resuscitate" tattooed on his chest. Alas, medical assistance in dying has no provision for any form of advanced directive—no matter how explicit. It does not speak to those who fear the transition of their mental capacities signaled by Alzheimer's or early onset of dementia. In a similar manner, it does not allow for living will directives, which would come into play if the patient suffered a traumatic injury that rendered them nonresponsive. Clearly, such directives could be open to even more confusion and coercion than is currently the case with medical assistance in dying, but if we are prepared to grant do not resuscitate directives for our aged parents, how more difficult would it be to give medical assistance in dying directives under controlled circumstances?

2. One consistent criticism of the legislation is not what it outlines and permits but the basis upon which it is made in the first place: a comprehensive system of palliative care. In some

communities, it is well developed and respected and acts as a firm foundation upon which to allow for medical assistance in dying. In other locations (both urban and rural) palliative care is spotty or nonexistent. Until palliative care becomes a universally available service, medical assistance in dying will be less than ideal as a tool in healing death.

A Funeral Rehearsal

This brief story came to me in the early stages of my field research.[6]

Bill's dad, Bob, was dying. There had be no reprieve from the cancer that was going to kill him, and a family gathering that was planned for Labor Day weekend was moved forward to the civic holiday in August.

Joking about the preparations for the arrival of the family, Bob suggested to his son that they post a sign over the living room: "Funeral Rehearsal." And that was in fact what happened. The close friends and family sat around Bob and "rehearsed" their eulogies, heartfelt memories, and lasting remembrances. It was a life-changing event. Bob was able to hear his children and grandchildren tell him how much he had done: the differences and miracles that had happened because of him. And those who gave gratitude to Bob were able to know that he now knew how they felt. A granddaughter would take away a life memory that she had told her grandfather how much he was loved. And she could rest in the knowledge that he had heard her. This kind of closure is rare. How wise were Bob and his family!

Everyone should have a funeral rehearsal.

Such events have always been theoretically possible, and it is testament to our lack of imagination or courage that we have not instituted a practice of a hosting a pre-funeral memorial service for those who are dying. Medical assistance in dying makes such pre-death celebrations/funerals more feasible and realistic. There

---

6. This story was told to me by Bill Elliott at a meeting on April 5, 2017, 11:30 AM.

had always been the uncertainty that if one held such an event, the patient might recover and live long past expectations. In that case, the funeral rehearsal might seem both morbid and a bit presumptuous. But with medical assistance in dying, we now have a firm date. There is time to plan. Friends and family can plan travel and iron out disturbing dynamics.

This story has been repeated often. For those who have given thought to how to end life, the ritual of gathering, the sharing of prayers and stories is a miracle cure. So many can find peace.

As was the case with Bob, giving time for families to ritualize their grief and offer gratitude to the loved one before they die is a great step forward in the healing process. How can we not take advantage of this gift of time to bring about the healing of the illness of death?

Appendix 1

DEFINITION OF ALS[1]

ALS is a motor neuron disease, also spelled "motor neurone disease," which is a group of neurological disorders that selectively affect motor neurons, the cells that control voluntary muscles of the body, including amyotrophic lateral sclerosis (ALS), primary lateral sclerosis, progressive muscular atrophy, progressive bulbar palsy, pseudobulbar palsy, and spinal muscular atrophy.

ALS itself can be classified a few different ways: by how fast the disease progresses (slow vs fast progressors), by whether it is inherited or sporadic, and by where it starts. Most commonly (~70 percent of the time) the limbs are affected first. In this case, neurons in the brain (upper motor neurons) and in the spinal cord (lower motor neurons) are dying and this form is called "limb onset." In about 25 percent of cases, muscles in the face, mouth, and throat are affected first because motor neurons in the part of the brain stem called the medulla oblongata (formerly called the "bulb") start to die first along with lower motor neurons. This form is called "bulbar onset." In about 5 percent of cases muscles in the trunk of the body are affected first. In all cases the disease spreads and affects other regions. The symptoms may also be limited to one spinal region.

1. See "Amyotrophic Lateral Sclerosis."

APPENDIX 1

Those with leg amyotrophic diplegia and brachial amyotrophic diplegia have a longer survival compared to classic onset ALS.

Signs and symptoms

The disorder causes muscle weakness and atrophy throughout the body due to the degeneration of the upper and lower motor neurons. Individuals affected by the disorder may ultimately lose the ability to initiate and control all voluntary movement, although bladder and bowel function and the muscles responsible for eye movement are usually spared until the final stages of the disorder.

Cognitive or behavioral dysfunction is present in up to half of individuals with ALS. Around half of people with ALS will experience mild changes in cognition and behavior, and 10–15 percent will show signs of frontotemporal dementia. Repeating phrases or gestures, apathy, and loss of inhibition are frequently reported behavioral features of ALS. Language dysfunction, executive dysfunction, and troubles with social cognition and verbal memory are the most commonly reported cognitive symptoms in ALS; a meta-analysis found no relationship between dysfunction and disease severity. However, cognitive and behavioral dysfunctions have been found to correlate with reduced survival in people with ALS and increased caregiver burden; this may be due in part to deficits in social cognition. About half the people who have ALS experience emotional lability, in which they cry or laugh for no reason.

Sensory nerves and the autonomic nervous system are generally unaffected, meaning the majority of people with ALS maintain hearing, sight, touch, smell, and taste.

Initial symptoms

The start of ALS may be so subtle that the symptoms are overlooked. The earliest symptoms of ALS are muscle weakness or muscle atrophy. Other presenting symptoms include trouble swallowing or breathing, cramping, or stiffness of affected muscles; muscle weakness affecting an arm or a leg; or slurred and nasal speech. The parts of the body affected by early symptoms of ALS depend on which motor neurons in the body are damaged first.

In limb-onset ALS, people first experience awkwardness when walking or running or even tripping over or stumbling may be experienced and often this is marked by walking with a "dropped foot" which drags gently on the ground. Or if arm-onset, difficulty with tasks requiring manual dexterity such as buttoning a shirt, writing, or turning a key in a lock may be experienced.

In bulbar-onset ALS, initial symptoms will mainly be of difficulty speaking clearly or swallowing. Speech may become slurred, nasal in character, or quieter. There may be difficulty in swallowing and loss of tongue mobility. A smaller proportion of people experience "respiratory-onset" ALS, where the intercostal muscles that support breathing are affected first.

Over time, people experience increasing difficulty moving, swallowing (dysphagia), and speaking or forming words (dysarthria). Symptoms of upper motor neuron involvement include tight and stiff muscles (spasticity) and exaggerated reflexes (hyperreflexia) including an overactive gag reflex. An abnormal reflex commonly called Babinski's sign also indicates upper motor neuron damage. Symptoms of lower motor neuron degeneration include muscle weakness and atrophy, muscle cramps, and fleeting twitches of muscles that can be seen under the skin (fasciculations) although twitching is not a diagnostic symptom and more of a side effect so twitching would either occur after or accompany weakness and atrophy.

Progression

Although the order and rate of symptoms vary from person to person, the disease eventually spreads to unaffected regions and the affected regions become more affected. Most people eventually are not able to walk or use their hands and arms, lose the ability to speak and swallow food and their own saliva, and begin to lose the ability to cough and to breathe on their own.

The rate of progression can be measured using an outcome measure called the "ALS Functional Rating Scale Revised (ALSFRS-R)," a twelve-item instrument administered as a clinical interview or self-reported questionnaire that produces a score between forty-eight (normal function) and zero (severe disability); it is the most commonly used outcome measure in clinical trials and is used by doctors to track disease progression. Though the degree of variability is high and a small percentage of people have a much slower disorder, on average, people with ALS lose about 0.9 FRS points per month. A survey-based study amongst clinicians showed that they rated a 20 percent change in the slope of the ALSFRS-R as being clinically meaningful.

Disorder progression tends to be slower in people who are younger than forty at onset, are mildly obese, have disorder restricted primarily to one limb, and those with primarily upper motor neuron symptoms. Conversely, progression is faster and prognosis poorer in people with bulbar-onset disorder, respiratory-onset disorder, and frontotemporal dementia.

The *CX3CR1* allelic variants have also been shown to have an effect on the disorder's progression and life expectancy.

Late stages

Difficulty in chewing and swallowing makes eating very difficult and increases the risk of choking or of aspirating food into the lungs. In later stages of the disorder, aspiration pneumonia can develop, and maintaining a healthy weight can become a significant problem that may require the insertion of a feeding tube. As the diaphragm and intercostal muscles of the rib cage that support breathing weaken, measures of lung function such as vital capacity and inspiratory pressure diminish. In respiratory-onset ALS, this may occur before significant limb weakness is apparent. Most people with ALS die of respiratory failure or pneumonia.

DEFINITION OF ALS

Although respiratory support can ease problems with breathing and prolong survival, it does not affect the progression of ALS. Most people with ALS die between two and four years after the diagnosis. Around half of people with ALS die within thirty months of their symptoms beginning, and about 20 percent of people with ALS live between five years and ten years after symptoms begin. Guitarist Jason Becker has lived since 1989 with the disorder, while physicist Stephen Hawking has survived for more than fifty years, but they are considered unusual cases.

Most people with ALS die in their own home, with their breath failing while they sleep; people rarely choke to death.

Appendix 2

BILL C-14

An Act to amend the Criminal Code and to make related amendments to other Acts (medical assistance in dying)

[*Assented to 17th June, 2016*]

Preamble

Whereas the Parliament of Canada recognizes the autonomy of persons who have a grievous and irremediable medical condition that causes them enduring and intolerable suffering and who wish to seek medical assistance in dying;

Whereas robust safeguards, reflecting the irrevocable nature of ending a life, are essential to prevent errors and abuse in the provision of medical assistance in dying;

Whereas it is important to affirm the inherent and equal value of every person's life and to avoid encouraging negative perceptions of the quality of life of persons who are elderly, ill or disabled;

Whereas vulnerable persons must be protected from being induced, in moments of weakness, to end their lives;

BILL C-14

Whereas suicide is a significant public health issue that can have lasting and harmful effects on individuals, families and communities;

Whereas, in light of the above considerations, permitting access to medical assistance in dying for competent adults whose deaths are reasonably foreseeable strikes the most appropriate balance between the autonomy of persons who seek medical assistance in dying, on one hand, and the interests of vulnerable persons in need of protection and those of society, on the other;

Whereas it is desirable to have a consistent approach to medical assistance in dying across Canada, while recognizing the provinces' jurisdiction over various matters related to medical assistance in dying, including the delivery of health care services and the regulation of health care professionals, as well as insurance contracts and coroners and medical examiners;

Whereas persons who avail themselves of medical assistance in dying should be able to do so without adverse legal consequences for their families—including the loss of eligibility for benefits—that would result from their death;

Whereas the Government of Canada has committed to uphold the principles set out in the *Canada Health Act*—public administration, comprehensiveness, universality, portability and accessibility—with respect to medical assistance in dying;

Whereas everyone has freedom of conscience and religion under section 2 of the *Canadian Charter of Rights and Freedoms*;

Whereas nothing in this Act affects the guarantee of freedom of conscience and religion;

Whereas the Government of Canada recognizes that in the living conditions of Canadians, there are diverse circumstances and that different groups have unique needs, and it commits to working with provinces, territories and civil society to facilitate access to palliative and end-of-life care, care and services for individuals living with Alzheimer's and dementia, appropriate mental health supports and services and culturally and spiritually appropriate end-of-life care for Indigenous patients;

And whereas the Government of Canada has committed to develop non-legislative measures that would support the improvement of a full range of options for end-of-life care, respect the personal convictions of health care providers and explore other situations—each having unique implications—in which a person may seek access to medical assistance in dying, namely situations giving rise to requests by mature minors, advance requests and requests where mental illness is the sole underlying medical condition;

Now, therefore, Her Majesty, by and with the advice and consent of the Senate and House of Commons of Canada, enacts as follows:

R.S., c. C-46

Criminal Code

1 Section 14 of the Criminal Code is replaced by the following:

Consent to death

14 No person is entitled to consent to have death inflicted on them, and such consent does not affect the criminal responsibility of any person who inflicts death on the person who gave consent.

2 The Act is amended by adding the following after section 226:

Exemption for medical assistance in dying

227 (1) No medical practitioner or nurse practitioner commits culpable homicide if they provide a person with medical assistance in dying in accordance with section 241.2.

Exemption for person aiding practitioner

(2) No person is a party to culpable homicide if they do anything for the purpose of aiding a medical practitioner or nurse practitioner to provide a person with medical assistance in dying in accordance with section 241.2.

BILL C-14

Reasonable but mistaken belief

(3) For greater certainty, the exemption set out in subsection (1) or (2) applies even if the person invoking it has a reasonable but mistaken belief about any fact that is an element of the exemption.

Non-application of section 14

(4) Section 14 does not apply with respect to a person who consents to have death inflicted on them by means of medical assistance in dying provided in accordance with section 241.2.

Definitions

(5) In this section, *medical assistance in dying*, *medical practitioner* and *nurse practitioner* have the same meanings as in section 241.1.

R.S., c. 27 (1st Supp.), s. 7(3)

3 Section 241 of the Act is replaced by the following:

Counselling or aiding suicide

241 (1) Everyone is guilty of an indictable offence and liable to imprisonment for a term of not more than 14 years who, whether suicide ensues or not,

- (a) counsels a person to die by suicide or abets a person in dying by suicide; or
- (b) aids a person to die by suicide.

Exemption for medical assistance in dying

(2) No medical practitioner or nurse practitioner commits an offence under paragraph (1)(b) if they provide a person with medical assistance in dying in accordance with section 241.2.

Exemption for person aiding practitioner

(3) No person is a party to an offence under paragraph (1)(b) if they do anything for the purpose of aiding a medical practitioner or nurse practitioner to provide a person with medical assistance in dying in accordance with section 241.2.

Exemption for pharmacist

(4) No pharmacist who dispenses a substance to a person other than a medical practitioner or nurse practitioner commits an offence under paragraph (1)(b) if the pharmacist dispenses the substance further to a prescription that is written by such a practitioner in providing medical assistance in dying in accordance with section 241.2.

Exemption for person aiding patient

(5) No person commits an offence under paragraph (1)(b) if they do anything, at another person's explicit request, for the purpose of aiding that other person to self-administer a substance that has been prescribed for that other person as part of the provision of medical assistance in dying in accordance with section 241.2.

Clarification

(5.1) For greater certainty, no social worker, psychologist, psychiatrist, therapist, medical practitioner, nurse practitioner or other health care professional commits an offence if they provide information to a person on the lawful provision of medical assistance in dying.

Reasonable but mistaken belief

(6) For greater certainty, the exemption set out in any of subsections (2) to (5) applies even if the person invoking the exemption has a reasonable but mistaken belief about any fact that is an element of the exemption.

Definitions

(7) In this section, *medical assistance in dying*, *medical practitioner*, *nurse practitioner* and *pharmacist* have the same meanings as in section 241.1.

Medical Assistance in Dying

Definitions

241.1 The following definitions apply in this section and in sections 241.2 to 241.4.

medical assistance in dying means

(a) the administering by a medical practitioner or nurse practitioner of a substance to a person, at their request, that causes their death; or

(b) the prescribing or providing by a medical practitioner or nurse practitioner of a substance to a person, at their request, so that they may self-administer the substance and in doing so cause their own death. (*aide médicale à mourir*)

medical practitioner means a person who is entitled to practise medicine under the laws of a province. (*médecin*)

nurse practitioner means a registered nurse who, under the laws of a province, is entitled to practise as a nurse practitioner—or under an equivalent designation—and to autonomously make diagnoses, order and interpret diagnostic tests, prescribe substances and treat patients. (*infirmier praticien*)

pharmacist means a person who is entitled to practise pharmacy under the laws of a province. (*pharmacien*)

Eligibility for medical assistance in dying

241.2 (1) A person may receive medical assistance in dying only if they meet all of the following criteria:

(a) they are eligible—or, but for any applicable minimum period of residence or waiting period, would be eligible—for health services funded by a government in Canada;

(b) they are at least 18 years of age and capable of making decisions with respect to their health;

(c) they have a grievous and irremediable medical condition;

(d) they have made a voluntary request for medical assistance in dying that, in particular, was not made as a result of external pressure; and

(e) they give informed consent to receive medical assistance in dying after having been informed of the means that are available to relieve their suffering, including palliative care.

Grievous and irremediable medical condition

(2) A person has a grievous and irremediable medical condition only if they meet all of the following criteria:

(a) they have a serious and incurable illness, disease or disability;

(b) they are in an advanced state of irreversible decline in capability;

(c) that illness, disease or disability or that state of decline causes them enduring physical or psychological suffering that is intolerable to them and that cannot be relieved under conditions that they consider acceptable; and

(d) their natural death has become reasonably foreseeable, taking into account all of their medical circumstances, without a prognosis necessarily having been made as to the specific length of time that they have remaining.

Safeguards

(3) Before a medical practitioner or nurse practitioner provides a person with medical assistance in dying, the medical practitioner or nurse practitioner must

(a) be of the opinion that the person meets all of the criteria set out in subsection (1);

(b) ensure that the person's request for medical assistance in dying was

(i) made in writing and signed and dated by the person or by another person under subsection (4), and

(ii) signed and dated after the person was informed by a medical practitioner or nurse practitioner that the person has a grievous and irremediable medical condition;

(c) be satisfied that the request was signed and dated by the person—or by another person under subsection (4)—before two independent witnesses who then also signed and dated the request;

(d) ensure that the person has been informed that they may, at any time and in any manner, withdraw their request;

(e) ensure that another medical practitioner or nurse practitioner has provided a written opinion confirming that the person meets all of the criteria set out in subsection (1);

(f) be satisfied that they and the other medical practitioner or nurse practitioner referred to in paragraph (e) are independent;

(g) ensure that there are at least 10 clear days between the day on which the request was signed by or on behalf of the person and the day on which the medical assistance in dying is provided or—if they and the other medical practitioner or nurse practitioner referred to in paragraph (e) are both of the opinion that the person's death, or the loss of their capacity to provide informed consent, is imminent—any shorter period that the first medical practitioner or nurse practitioner considers appropriate in the circumstances;

(h) immediately before providing the medical assistance in dying, give the person an opportunity to withdraw their request and ensure that the person gives express consent to receive medical assistance in dying; and

(i) if the person has difficulty communicating, take all necessary measures to provide a reliable means by which the person may understand the information that is provided to them and communicate their decision.

APPENDIX 2

Unable to sign

(4) If the person requesting medical assistance in dying is unable to sign and date the request, another person—who is at least 18 years of age, who understands the nature of the request for medical assistance in dying and who does not know or believe that they are a beneficiary under the will of the person making the request, or a recipient, in any other way, of a financial or other material benefit resulting from that person's death—may do so in the person's presence, on the person's behalf and under the person's express direction.

Independent witness

(5) Any person who is at least 18 years of age and who understands the nature of the request for medical assistance in dying may act as an independent witness, except if they

    (a) know or believe that they are a beneficiary under the will of the person making the request, or a recipient, in any other way, of a financial or other material benefit resulting from that person's death;

    (b) are an owner or operator of any health care facility at which the person making the request is being treated or any facility in which that person resides;

    (c) are directly involved in providing health care services to the person making the request; or

    (d) directly provide personal care to the person making the request.

Independence—medical practitioners and nurse practitioners

(6) The medical practitioner or nurse practitioner providing medical assistance in dying and the medical practitioner or nurse practitioner who provides the opinion referred to in paragraph (3)(e) are independent if they

    (a) are not a mentor to the other practitioner or responsible for supervising their work;

(b) do not know or believe that they are a beneficiary under the will of the person making the request, or a recipient, in any other way, of a financial or other material benefit resulting from that person's death, other than standard compensation for their services relating to the request; or

(c) do not know or believe that they are connected to the other practitioner or to the person making the request in any other way that would affect their objectivity.

Reasonable knowledge, care and skill

(7) Medical assistance in dying must be provided with reasonable knowledge, care and skill and in accordance with any applicable provincial laws, rules or standards.

Informing pharmacist

(8) The medical practitioner or nurse practitioner who, in providing medical assistance in dying, prescribes or obtains a substance for that purpose must, before any pharmacist dispenses the substance, inform the pharmacist that the substance is intended for that purpose.

Clarification

(9) For greater certainty, nothing in this section compels an individual to provide or assist in providing medical assistance in dying.

Failure to comply with safeguards

241.3 A medical practitioner or nurse practitioner who, in providing medical assistance in dying, knowingly fails to comply with all of the requirements set out in paragraphs 241.2(3)(b) to (i) and subsection 241.2(8) is guilty of an offence and is liable

(a) on conviction on indictment, to a term of imprisonment of not more than five years; or

(b) on summary conviction, to a term of imprisonment of not more than 18 months.

APPENDIX 2

Forgery

241.4 (1) Everyone commits an offence who commits forgery in relation to a request for medical assistance in dying.

Destruction of documents

(2) Everyone commits an offence who destroys a document that relates to a request for medical assistance in dying with intent to interfere with

- (a) another person's access to medical assistance in dying;
- (b) the lawful assessment of a request for medical assistance in dying; or
- (c) another person invoking an exemption under any of subsections 227(1) or (2), 241(2) to (5) or 245(2).

Punishment

(3) Everyone who commits an offence under subsection (1) or (2) is liable

- (a) on conviction on indictment, to a term of imprisonment of not more than five years; or
- (b) on summary conviction, to a term of imprisonment of not more than 18 months.

Definition of *document*

(4) In subsection (2), *document* has the same meaning as in section 321.

4 The Act is amended by adding the following after section 241.3:

Filing information—medical practitioner or nurse practitioner

241.31 (1) Unless they are exempted under regulations made under subsection (3), a medical practitioner or nurse practitioner who receives a written request for medical assistance in dying must, in accordance with those regulations, provide the information required by those regulations to the recipient designated in those regulations.

Filing information—pharmacist

(2) Unless they are exempted under regulations made under subsection (3), a pharmacist who dispenses a substance in connection with the provision of medical assistance in dying must, in accordance with those regulations, provide the information required by those regulations to the recipient designated in those regulations.

Regulations

(3) The Minister of Health must make regulations that he or she considers necessary

    (a) respecting the provision and collection, for the purpose of monitoring medical assistance in dying, of information relating to requests for, and the provision of, medical assistance in dying, including

        (i) the information to be provided, at various stages, by medical practitioners or nurse practitioners and by pharmacists, or by a class of any of them,

        (ii) the form, manner and time in which the information must be provided,

        (iii) the designation of a person as the recipient of the information, and

        (iv) the collection of information from coroners and medical examiners;

    (b) respecting the use of that information, including its analysis and interpretation, its protection and its publication and other disclosure;

    (c) respecting the disposal of that information; and

    (d) exempting, on any terms that may be specified, a class of persons from the requirement set out in subsection (1) or (2).

APPENDIX 2

Guidelines—information on death certificates

(3.1) The Minister of Health, after consultation with representatives of the provincial governments responsible for health, must establish guidelines on the information to be included on death certificates in cases where medical assistance in dying has been provided, which may include the way in which to clearly identify medical assistance in dying as the manner of death, as well as the illness, disease or disability that prompted the request for medical assistance in dying.

Offence and punishment

(4) A medical practitioner or nurse practitioner who knowingly fails to comply with subsection (1), or a pharmacist who knowingly fails to comply with subsection (2),

- (a) is guilty of an indictable offence and liable to a term of imprisonment of not more than two years; or
- (b) is guilty of an offence punishable on summary conviction.

Offence and punishment

(5) Everyone who knowingly contravenes the regulations made under subsection (3)

- (a) is guilty of an indictable offence and liable to a term of imprisonment of not more than two years; or
- (b) is guilty of an offence punishable on summary conviction.

5 Subsection 241.4(2) of the Act is amended by striking out "or" at the end of paragraph (b), by adding "or" at the end of paragraph (c) and by adding the following after that paragraph:

- (d) the provision by a person of information under section 241.31.

BILL C-14

6 Section 245 of the Act is renumbered as subsection 245(1) and is amended by adding the following after that subsection:

Exemption

(2) Subsection (1) does not apply to

(a) a medical practitioner or nurse practitioner who provides medical assistance in dying in accordance with section 241.2; and

(b) a person who does anything for the purpose of aiding a medical practitioner or nurse practitioner to provide medical assistance in dying in accordance with section 241.2.

Definitions

(3) In subsection (2), *medical assistance in dying*, *medical practitioner* and *nurse practitioner* have the same meanings as in section 241.1.

Related Amendments

R.S., c. P-6

Pension Act

7 (1) The definition improper conduct in subsection 3(1) of the Pension Act is replaced by the following:

improper conduct includes wilful disobedience of orders, vicious or criminal conduct and wilful self-inflicted wounding—except if the wound results from the receipt of medical assistance in dying and the requirement set out in paragraph 241.2(3)(a) of the *Criminal Code* has been met; (*mauvaise conduite*)

(2) Subsection 3(1) of the Act is amended by adding the following in alphabetical order:

medical assistance in dying has the same meaning as in section 241.1 of the *Criminal Code*; (*aide médicale à mourir*)

(3) Section 3 of the Act is amended by adding the following after subsection (3):

Deeming—medical assistance in dying

(4) For the purposes of this Act, if a member of the forces receives medical assistance in dying, that member is deemed to have died as a result of the illness, disease or disability for which they were determined to be eligible to receive that assistance, in accordance with paragraph 241.2(3)(a) of the *Criminal Code*.

1992, c. 20

Corrections and Conditional Release Act

8 Section 19 of the *Corrections and Conditional Release Act* is amended by adding the following after subsection (1):

Medical assistance in dying

(1.1) Subsection (1) does not apply to a death that results from an inmate receiving *medical assistance in dying*, as defined in section 241.1 of the *Criminal Code*, in accordance with section 241.2 of that Act.

2005, c. 21

BILL C-14

Canadian Forces Members and Veterans Re-establishment and Compensation Act

9 (1) Subsection 2(1) of the *Canadian Forces Members and Veterans Re-establishment and Compensation Act* is amended by adding the following in alphabetical order:

medical assistance in dying has the same meaning as in section 241.1 of the *Criminal Code*. (*aide médicale à mourir*)

(2) Section 2 of the Act is amended by adding the following after subsection (5):

Interpretation—medical assistance in dying

(6) For the purposes of this Act, a member or veteran has neither inflicted wilful self-injury nor engaged in improper conduct by reason only that they receive medical assistance in dying, if the requirement set out in paragraph 241.2(3)(a) of the *Criminal Code* has been met.

Deeming—medical assistance in dying

(7) For the purposes of this Act, if a member or a veteran receives medical assistance in dying, that member or veteran is deemed to have died as a result of the illness, disease or disability for which they were determined to be eligible to receive that assistance, in accordance with paragraph 241.2(3)(a) of the *Criminal Code*.

Independent Review

Mature minors, advance requests and mental illness

9.1 (1) The Minister of Justice and the Minister of Health must, no later than 180 days after the day on which this Act receives royal assent, initiate one or more independent reviews of issues relating to requests by mature minors for medical assistance in dying, to advance requests and to requests where mental illness is the sole underlying medical condition.

APPENDIX 2

(2) The Minister of Justice and the Minister of Health must, no later than two years after the day on which a review is initiated, cause one or more reports on the review, including any findings or recommendations resulting from it, to be laid before each House of Parliament.

Review of Act

Review by committee

10 (1) At the start of the fifth year after the day on which this Act receives royal assent, the provisions enacted by this Act are to be referred to the committee of the Senate, of the House of Commons or of both Houses of Parliament that may be designated or established for the purpose of reviewing the provisions.

Report

(2) The committee to which the provisions are referred is to review them and the state of palliative care in Canada and submit a report to the House or Houses of Parliament of which it is a committee, including a statement setting out any changes to the provisions that the committee recommends.

Coming into Force

Order in council

11 Sections 4 and 5 come into force 12 months after the day on which this Act receives royal assent or on any earlier day that may be fixed by order of the Governor in Council.

Published under authority of the Speaker of the House of Commons

BIBLIOGRAPHY

Abdul-Khaaliq, Nashid. "Suicide and Islam: A Deeper Perspective." *Ascertain the Truth*, January 30, 2010. http://www.ascertainthetruth.com/att/index.php/al-islam/al-islam-and-suicide/131-suicide-and-islam-a-deeper-perspective/.

Adach, Kate. "'I Can Still Clearly Hear His Screams': Medically Assisted Dying Access Questioned." *CBC News*, June 18, 2017. https://www.cbc.ca/news/canada/calgary/medically-assisted-dying-calls-1.4166707.

Albom, Mitchell. *Tuesdays with Morrie: An Old Man, a Young Man, and Life's Greatest Lesson*. New York: Random, 1997.

"Amyotrophic Lateral Sclerosis." Wikipedia, June 8, 2020. https://en.wikipedia.org/wiki/Amyotrophic_lateral_sclerosis.

Barnard, Christiaan. *Good Life, Good Death: A Doctor's Case for Euthanasia and Suicide*. Englewood Cliffs, NJ: Prentice-Hall, 1980.

"Bill C-14." OpenParliament.ca, 42nd Parliament, 1st Session. https://openparliament.ca/bills/42-1/C-14/.

Blackwell, Tom. "B.C. Man Faced Excruciating Transfer After Catholic Hospital Refused Assisted-Death Request." *National Post*, September 27, 2016. https://nationalpost.com/news/canada/b-c-man-faced-excruciating-transfer-after-catholic-hospital-refused-assisted-death-request.

Brown, Raymond. *The Birth of the Messiah: A Commentary on the Infancy Narratives in the Gospels of Matthew and Luke*. New York: Doubleday, 1979.

Cayley, Arthur, the Younger, ed. *Memoirs of Sir Thomas More, &c*. Vol 2. London: Cadell and Davis, 1808.

Dickens, Charles. *A Christmas Carol*. Stave 3. Dover Thrift Edition. New York: Dover, 1991.

Gawande, Atul. *Being Mortal: Medicine and What Happens In the End*. Toronto: Canada Doubleday, 2014.

Hall, Douglas John. *Professing the Faith: Christian Theology in a North American Context*. Minneapolis: Fortress, 1993.

BIBLIOGRAPHY

———. *The Steward: A Biblical Symbol Come of Age*. New York: Friendship, 1982.

Hasham, Alyshah. "77-Year-Old Seeks Court Declaration to Allow Her Medically-Assisted Death." *The Star*, June 18, 2017. https://www.thestar.com/news/gta/2017/06/18/77-year-old-seeks-court-declaration-to-allow-her-medically-assisted-death.html.

"Hippocratic Oath." Wikipedia. https://en.wikipedia.org/wiki/Hippocratic_Oath.

"Issues in Jewish Ethics: Suicide." Jewish Virtual Library, n.d. http://www.jewishvirtuallibrary.org/suicide-in-judaism.

Kelly, Eugene. *Chasing Daylight: How My Forthcoming Death Transformed My Life*. New York: McGraw-Hill, 2006.

Kierkegaard, Soren. *Fear and Trembling*. n.p.: Feather Trail, 2009.

Levan, Christopher. "Conundrum: Can Forgiveness Be Forced?" *United Church Observer*, September 2017. http://preview.ucobserver.org/columns/2017/09/conundrums_sept2017/.

Miller, Robert, ed. *The Complete Gospels*. Sonoma, CA: Polebridge, 1992.

More, Thomas. *Utopia*, New York: Penguin Classics, 2003.

Ogilvie, Kelvin Kenneth, and Robert Oliphant. "Medical Assistance in Dying: A Patient-Centered Approach." Report of the Special Joint Committee on Physician-Assisted Dying, 42nd Parliament, 1st Session. February 2016. https://www.parl.ca/DocumentViewer/en/42-1/PDAM/report-1.

O'Neill, Eugene. *The Last Will and Testament of an Extremely Distinguished Dog*. Carlisle, MA: Applewood, 2014.

Salt Spring Island Foundation. "Salt Spring Island's Vital Signs, 2017." https://ssifoundation.ca/wp-content/uploads/2017/10/SSIF-Vital-Signs-Report.pdf.

Short, Michael. "Why Australia Should Allow the Right to Physician-Assisted Death." *The Age*, March 22, 2016. https://www.theage.com.au/opinion/why-australia-should-allow-the-right-to-physicianassisted-death-20160322-gnoaro.html.

Thomas, Dylan. "Do Not Go Gentle Into That Good Night." *Botteghe Oscure* (1951).

United Church of Canada. "Medical Assistance in Dying." Executive of the General Council, May 6–7, 2017. https://commons.united-church.ca/Documents/What%20We%20Believe%20and%20Why/Death%20and%20Dying/Medical%20Assistance%20in%20Dying.pdf.

———. "United Church Opts for a Balanced, Case-by-Case Approach to Medical Assistance in Dying." May 8, 2017. https://www.united-church.ca/news/medical-assistance-dying.

Yoder, John. *When War Is Unjust: Being Honest in Just-War Thinking*. Eugene, OR: Wipf and Stock, 1996.

www.ingramcontent.com/pod-product-compliance
Lightning Source LLC
Chambersburg PA
CBHW032232080426
42735CB00008B/820